MW01598737

EXCEEDINGLY NIETZSCHE

WARWICK STUDIES IN PHILOSOPHY AND LITERATURE
General editor: David Wood

It used to be commonplace to insist on the elimination of the 'literary' dimension from philosophy. This was particularly true for a philosophical tradition inspired by the possibilities of formalization and by the success of the natural sciences. And yet even in the most rigorous instances of such philosophy we find demands for 'clarity', for 'tight' argument, and distinctions between 'strong' and 'weak' proofs which call out for a rhetorical reading. Equally, modern literary theory, quite as much as literature itself, is increasingly looking to philosophy (and other theoretical disciplines such as linguistics) for its inspiration. After a wave of structuralist analysis, the growing influence of deconstructive and hermeneutic readings continues to bear witness to this. While philosophy and literature are not to be identified, even if philosophy is thought of as 'a kind of writing', much of the most exciting theoretical work being done today, in Britain, Europe and America, exploits their tensions and intertwinings. When one recalls that Plato, who wished to keep philosophy and poetry apart, actually unified the two in his own writing, it is clear that the current upsurge of interest in this field is only reengaging with the questions alive in the broader tradition.

The University of Warwick pioneered the undergraduate study of the theoretical coition of Philosophy and Literature, and its recently established Centre for Research in Philosophy and Literature has won wide acclaim for its adventurous and dynamic programme of conferences and research. With this Series the work of the Centre is opened to a wider public. Each volume aims to bring the best scholarship to bear on topical themes in an atmosphere of intellectual excitement. The series will be further developed by the inclusion of monographs by distinguished academics.

EXCEEDINGLY NIETZSCHE

*Aspects of Contemporary
Nietzsche-Interpretation*

Edited by
DAVID FARRELL KRELL
and
DAVID WOOD

ROUTLEDGE
London and New York

First published in 1988 by
Routledge
11 New Fetter Lane, London EC4P 4EE

Published in the USA by
Routledge & Kegan Paul Inc.
in association with Methuen Inc.
29 West 35th Street, New York, NY 10001

Set in 10 on 12 point Sabon
by Columns of Reading
and printed in Great Britain
by T.J. Press (Padstow) Ltd
Padstow, Cornwall

Library of Congress Cataloging in Publication Data

Exceedingly Nietzsche: aspects of contemporary Nietzsche
– interpretation / edited by David Farrell Krell and David Wood.
p. cm. – (Warwick studies in philosophy and literature: vol. 1)
Includes index.
1. Nietzsche, Friedrich Wilhelm, 1844–1900. I. Krell, David Farrell.
II. Wood, David (David C.) III. Series.
B3317.E89 1988
193–dc19   87–18615

British Library CIP Data also available
ISBN 0–415–00189–7

Contents

Contents

Notes on the Contributors

ALISON AINLEY is a graduate student in the Department of Philosophy at the University of Warwick, where she is currently working on a thesis on feminism and ethics. She has written on Levinas and Kristeva in *The Provocation of Levinas* (forthcoming) and has poems included in *The Eric Gregory Anthology* (Salamander, 1987).

PETER DEWS is currently Lecturer in European Thought and Literature, in the Department of Humanities, Cambridgeshire College of Arts and Technology. He is the editor of an anthology of interviews with Jurgen Habermas, *Autonomy and Solidarity* (Verso 1986) and is the author of *Logics of Disintegration: Post-structuralist Thought and the Claims of Critical Theory* (Verso 1987).

MICHEL HAAR is *maître des conférences* at the University of Paris (Sorbonne). He has translated Nietzsche for the French edition of the *Gesamtausgabe* and has written many articles on contemporary philosophy, especially on Heidegger and Nietzsche. He is the author of *La Chant de la terre* (L'Herne, 1987).

DAVID FARRELL KRELL is Senior Lecturer and Chairman in the Department of Philosophy at the University of Essex. He is the author of *Intimations of Morality: Time, Truth and Finitude in*

Heidegger's Thinking of Being (Pennsylvania State University Press, 1986) and *Postponements: Woman, Sensuality, and Death in Nietzsche* (Indiana University Press, 1986) and the editor of a number of Heidegger's works in English, including the multivolume *Nietzsche*.

ALPHONSO LINGIS is Professor of Philosophy at Pennsylvania State University. He is the author of *Excesses: Eros and Culture* (New York, SUNY Press, 1983), *Libido: The French Existential Theories* (Indiana University Press, 1986) and *Phenomenological Explanations* (Martinus Nijhoff, 1986). He has also translated six works of Merleau-Ponty, Levinas and Janicaud.

DAVID POLLARD lives and works in Sussex. He specializes in the philosophy of language and is the author of *The Poetry of Keats: Language and Experience.*

JOHN SALLIS is Schmitt Professor of Philosophy at Loyola University of Chicago. His books include *Phenomenology and the Return to Beginnings, Being and Logos, The Gathering of Reason, Delimitations*, and *Spacings – of Reason and Imagination.* He is founding editor of *Research in Phenomenology.*

ALAN D. SCHRIFT teaches philosophy and humanities at Grinnell College, Grinnell, Iowa. He has published a number of articles on Nietzsche, Heidegger and Derrida, is co-editor of *Hermeneutics and Post Modern Theories of Interpretation* and is completing a manuscript on Heidegger, Derrida and Deleuze's readings of Nietzsche.

HUGH TOMLINSON is a writer and translator based in London. He has translated a number of books by Giles Deleuze, including *Nietzsche and Philosophy*; *Kant's Critical Philosophy*; *Cinema I: the Movement-Image* and *Dialogues.* He is a member of the

Second of January Group and has recently published, among other writings, several discussions of post-modernism.

DAVID WOOD teaches philosophy at the University of Warwick. He is author of *The Deconstruction of Time* (1988); *Philosophy and Style* (1988); and editor or co-editor of *Heidegger and Language* (1981); *Time and Metaphysics* (1982); and *Derrida and Différance* (1985), all with Parousia Press. He has published numerous papers in the field of continental philosophy, particularly on Time and on Derrida. He is Programme Director of Warwick's Centre for Research in Philosophy and Literature.

Preface

Friedrich Nietzsche in Turin to Jacob Burckhardt in Basle, postmarked 6 January 1889:

Dear Professor,
  In the end I would far rather be a Basle professor than God. But I did not dare on that account push my personal egoism so far as to leave the creation of the world undone. You see, one has to make sacrifices, depending on how and where one lives . . .
  What is unpleasant – and it diminishes my modesty – is the fact that at bottom every name of history I am.
  With heartfelt love,
  Yours,
  Nietzsche
  Tomorrow my son Umberto is coming with the lovely Margerita, whom I also receive here, quite simply, in my shirtsleeves. The rest for Frau Cosima . . . Ariadne . . . From time to time all is magic.

In the new critical edition of Nietzsche's correspondence (Berlin, 1975 ff.) the letter from which these extracts are taken (number 1,256) is cited as Nietzsche's very last. Its excesses are many: the elevation to divine status, a status inferior only to that of a Basle professorship; the creation of the universe as an act of *noblesse oblige* and personal sacrifice; and the identification with every name in history, an identification in which the very syntax of the language is distorted: *daß im Grunde jeder Name in der Geschichte ich bin.* And yet it is all yoked by *irony* and by a certain *control* exercised by the rhetoric, releasing itself only to the figure of Ariadne. Beyond the names of history, the names of enchantment: *Von Zeit zu Zeit wird gezaubert.* Both the overflow and the control, the transport and the destination, the trance and the irony, both the transhistorical exultation and the unstinting identification with history are exceedingly Nietzsche.

The history of Nietzsche-interpretation in the past twenty-five years is already exceedingly complex: we will not even try to sketch it here. The Warwick Workshop in Continental Philosophy for the year 1984 was quite consciously designed to reflect as many aspects of Nietzsche in contemporary philosophy, literature and the social sciences as possible. Nevertheless, the interests of the participants seem in retrospect to have fallen rather neatly into two general areas – whence the two parts of the present collection.

In Part One, 'Music, Madness and Metaphysics', the papers focus on Nietzsche at the limit of the metaphysical tradition. John Sallis traces the elusive and explosive figure of Nietzsche's Dionysus as it exceeds conceptual grasp, exceeds metaphysics; Michel Haar examines Heidegger's hesitation before the 'madness of the body' in Nietzsche's physiology of artistic creativity; David Wood locates Nietzsche's exceeding of metaphysics in the transvaluative thought of time as eternal recurrence of the same; David Pollard examines the excesses, antagonisms and attempted reconciliations that William Blake and Nietzsche to an astonishing degree share; finally, David Farrell Krell traces certain familial excesses in Nietzsche's accounts of his mother and sister, his father and little brother, the last two involving excesses of music.

In Part Two, 'Women, Men and Machines of War', the focus is on the cutting edge of Nietzsche's thought – his genealogical critique, as taken up in the work of a number of contemporary thinkers, particularly in France. Alphonso Lingis, taking his inspiration from remarks of Nietzsche's on the body as artwork and on the corruptibility of the artist, analyses the contemporary cult and ancient rites of body-building; Alison Ainley elaborates a reading of the Nietzschean/Derridean metaphor of 'woman', unfolding in a positive way the seductions of fecundity and pregnancy; Alan D. Schrift discusses the multiple senses of the 'end' of 'man' in two devoted readers of Nietzsche: Foucault and Derrida; Hugh Tomlinson debates the question of the vulnerability of Gilles Deleuze's systematic account of genealogical critique in *Nietzsche and Philosophy*, as well as in his and Félix Guattari's more recent work; finally, Peter Dews attempts to guide recent post-structuralist accounts of genealogy back to the social-critical thought of T. W. Adorno, by means of a guideline which stretches from Schelling's 'absolute Indifference' to Derrida's 'différance'.

Not all the papers presented here were read at the 1984 Workshop: those of Alison Ainley, Alphonso Lingis and Michel Haar came to our attention after the event. Each would have been a welcome addition at that time, and we are delighted that they shall join the discussion now.

We owe debts of gratitude to the authors of the papers, who have not ceased to revise and to refine them since the time of the Workshop; and to Tamra Wright for her help at each stage of the book's production. Sarah Richmond kindly compiled the index.

D.F.K.
D.C.W.

Abbreviations

Nietzsche's works will be cited throughout according to the following abbreviations. Naturally, the authors used various editions and translations, so uniformity could not be guaranteed except in the case of reference to the paragraphs and aphorisms of Nietzsche's own individual publications.

GT   *Die Geburt der Tragödie* [*The Birth of Tragedy*], 1872

UB I–IV   *Unzeitgemässe Betrachtungen* [*Untimely Meditations*], 1873–76

MA   *Menschliches, Allzumenschliches* [*Human, All Too Human*], 1878–80

M   *Morgenröte* [*Daybreak*], 1881

FW   *Die fröhliche Wissenschaft* [*The Gay Science*], 1882

ASZ I–IV   *Also sprach Zarathustra* [*Thus Spoke Zarathustra*], 1883–85

JGB   *Jenseits von Gut und Böse* [*Beyond Good and Evil*], 1886

ZGM I–III   *Zur Genealogie der Moral* [*On The Genealogy of Morals*], 1887

GD   *Götzen-Dämmerung* [*Twilight of the Idols*], [1888], 1889

AC   *Der Antichrist* [*The Antichrist*], [1888], 1895

EH   *Ecce Homo*, [1888], 1908

DD   *Dionysos-Dithyramben* [*Dithyrambs of Dionysus*], [1888–89], 1891

WM   *Der Wille Zur Macht* [*The Will to Power*], 1901*

* This volume is included here for ease of reference, although the posthumous editorial processes of which it is a product make it a less than reliable Nietzschean text.

· PART ONE ·

MUSIC, MADNESS AND METAPHYSICS

· 1 ·

Dionysus – In Excess of Metaphysics

JOHN SALLIS

I shall be concerned with a figure, one that is different from most, perhaps from almost all, others; a figure drawn, or rather withdrawn, in such a manner that it can have no direct image, even though, on the other hand, it can become, in its way, manifest. This figure could be considered the most perfectly metaphysical, the original *an sich*, so compactly an original, so thoroughly *an sich*, as to withhold itself from direct disclosure in an image. And yet by virtue of this very withdrawing it can instead be considered a transgressive figure, a figure which veers off toward the limit of metaphysics, that exceeds metaphysics, a figure in excess of metaphysics. The name of the figure is *Dionysus*. The text in which the figure is drawn: Nietzsche's *The Birth of Tragedy*.[1]

Dionysis – in Euripides' *Bacchae* Pentheus declares him an impostor, a deceiver, a seducer. Yet such is his power that all the women of Thebes have flocked to Mt Kithairon to take part in the revels of the god; even those women whom Pentheus has had put in chains and thrown into the dungeon have escaped, the chains on their legs snapping apart, the doors of the dungeon swinging open. When Pentheus then imprisons the stranger in the darkness of the stables he discovers how hopeless it is to try to confine this Dionysian figure: an earthquake, shaking everything loose, leaves the entire palace in ruins. The stranger recounts exactly what happened when Pentheus sought to chain him: Pentheus suddenly found himself engaged in binding not the stranger but a bull;

3

instead of constraining the stranger, he ended up, ridiculously, trying to put a rope around the knees and hooves of the bull. Pentheus' outrage against the god is soon repaid in full: Pentheus is torn to pieces by the Dionysian throng, among whom is his own mother in a state of frenzy. Or again, in a Homeric hymn, Dionysus is seized by certain Tyrrhenian pirates who bind him as a slave only to find that the chains fall away, that he breaks all bonds, that he cannot be bound. Stories also abound concerning the practices of his votaries – stories, for example, of how the Maenads could tear goats or deer to pieces with their bare hands and then devour the raw flesh. But also stories of how, on the other hand, they demonstrated deep sympathy with the beasts, often suckling kids and fawns. The apparent contradiction disappears as soon as it is recognized that in both instances it is a matter of a disruption of the limits that would delimit the individual. In one instance it is a matter of exceeding those limits, that is, of a bond with what otherwise would be the other:

> Under the magic of the Dionysian not only is the bond between man and man reestablished, but nature which has become alienated, hostile, or subjugated, celebrates once more its reconciliation with its lost son, man. (§1)

In the other instance it is a matter of dissolution, of tearing to pieces, as Dionysus himself was each year torn to pieces by the Titans. It is a matter, on the one hand, of expanding the limit indefinitely and, on the other, of contracting it indefinitely – a matter of expanding or contracting indefinitely, that is, limitlessly – hence in both cases a matter of disrupting the limit.

Near the beginning of *The Birth of Tragedy*, Nietzsche schematizes the Dionysian in the most classical manner: the Dionysian is, first of all, one of the 'artistic energies which burst forth from nature itself *without the mediation of the human artist*' (§2). Thus it is a matter of dividing the Dionysian according to the classical opposition between nature and art and the classical concept of mimesis. There is, first of all, a natural Dionysian state which would then be mimetically reproduced in Dionysian art. Let us, for the moment, follow the lines of this classical schema and consider first the natural Dionysian state.

A note written in the Fall of 1869 provides a point of departure

Nietzsche writes: In those orgiastic festivals of Dionysus there prevailed such a degree of being-outside-oneself [*Ausser-sich-sein*], of *ekstasis*, that men acted and felt like transformed and enchanted beings.[2] Add to this a phrase from *The Birth of Tragedy*: Nietzsche writes of 'the rapture [*Verzückung*] of the Dionysian state with its annihilation of the ordinary bounds and limits of existence' (§7). The Dionysian state is, then, one of ecstasy, a state of being utterly outside oneself. And yet the concept, the figure, of being-outside-oneself releases a strange logic, especially if it is not stabilized by a dialectic of appropriation. In Dionysian ecstasy, in being-outside-oneself, one transgresses the limits that ordinarily would delimit one's self, one's individuality, one's subjectivity. These limits separating man from man and man from nature would be annihilated, and man would be reunited with both man and nature. The Maenads would mother all creatures, suckling even kids and fawns.

But kids and fawns were also torn to pieces by the Maenads, as Dionysus himself was each year torn to pieces by the Titans, and as Pentheus was torn to pieces by his own mother. The logic is such that, in transgressing the limits that would separate 'inside' from 'outside' – the limits that would delimit one's own subjectivity – one would also disrupt that delimitation. The 'inside' would not simply remain intact, but rather the subjective would vanish into *Selbstvergessenheit*: as Dionysian emotions 'grow in intensity the subjective vanishes into complete *Selbstvergessenheit*' (§1). More precisely, Dionysian ecstasy, being-outside-oneself, would be a matter not simply of relating an inside to an outside but rather of shifting the 'inside' into the 'outside', displacing it, disrupting the very logic of the opposition inside/outside. The Dionysian, this ecstasy bursting forth from nature itself, would be a deconstruction indeed of subjectivity.

Because it is sheer ecstasy, the Dionysian is utterly opposed to the other of those artistic energies which burst forth from nature itself, namely the Apollonian. In the Apollonian, especially in Apollonian art, beautiful images serve as transfiguring mirrors in which one appears to oneself more perfect, more complete, shining in a higher truth. In other words, in the Apollonian image one is given a measure by which to measure oneself, a measure by which to draw around oneself the limits of an individuality, even if one never entirely measures up to it. The drawing of this limit and the drawing of oneself into it constitute Apollonian self-knowledge.

But to this Apollonian measure the votaries of Dionysus oppose *excess* (*Übermaß*). Or rather, as ecstasy, the Dionysian state is excess itself, what one could call excess *as such*, were not such excess precisely such as to disrupt the very operation of delimitation that every 'as such' presupposes. It is the exceeding of any limit by which one's individuality would be delimited, by which the self would be defined and constituted as an interior space of self-possession. This exceeding, this being in excess of subjectivity, is at the same time the dissolution of subjectivity, the utter disruption of determinate selfhood, being torn to pieces. The Dionysian state is an abysmal loss of self, and this is why Nietzsche consistently relates it to terror, dread, suffering (*Schrecken, Entsetzlichkeit, Leiden*); not because the Dionysian state produces or discloses terror, dread, and suffering, but because the Dionysian is as such (I write here under erasure) that abysmal loss of self, loss of self-possession and its measure, that one undergoes in various degrees and in various connections when one is struck with terror, possessed by dread, or overcome with suffering.

In the history of Greece the Apollonian culture was overwhelmed by the intrusion of the Dionysian festival. Here is how Nietzsche describes this intrusion:

And now let us consider how this world built on appearance [*Schein*] and moderation [*Mäßigung*] and artificially dammed up, there rang out in every more alluring and magical ways the ecstatic sound of the Dionysian festival; how in these all of nature's *excess* (Übermaß] in pleasure, suffering, and knowledge became audible, even in piercing shrieks ... The muses of the arts of 'appearance' ['*Schein*'] paled before an art that, in its frenzy [*Rausch*], spoke the truth. The wisdom of Silenus cried 'Woe! woe!' to the serene Olympians. The individual, with all his limits and restraints [*mit allen seinen Grenzen und Maßen*] succumbed to the *Selbstvergessenheit* of the Dionysian states, forgetting the Apollonian precepts. *Excess* revealed itself as truth [*Das* Übermaß *enthüllte sich als Wahrheit*].

Knowledge audible in piercing shrieks, truth spoken in frenzy, wisdom heard in the cries of Silenus – the Dionysian festival is a revelation of excess as truth, or equally, of truth as excess. But excess, Dionysian *ekstasis*, is not simply a truth, not even a fundamental truth, not even the fundamental truth. One could of course undertake to stabilize the result of the revelation, asserting, for instance, that Dionysian excess underlies all things as their ground, as the origin from which they arise in their determinateness. But one could put forth such a formulation only by ignoring the way in which that would-be ground disrupts the very ordering that belongs to the concept of ground and dissolves the very determinateness that it would, as ground, produce. What the Dionysian revelation reveals is not a ground of determination but the dissolution of ground and of determination. What it reveals is not ground but rather – and I use the word very cautiously – abyss. Apollonian truth, the figure of Apollo in which the limits of individuation are drawn, the Olympian images in which one is reflected back to oneself, such truth can cover over the abysmal Dionysian truth but can never cease being threatened by it. Metaphysical truth too, as it comes into the world through Socrates, will be cast at the edge of the abyss, the drive for ground and determinateness diverting it from ecstatic exposure to the abyss. For more than two millenia, metaphysics will move within the space between beings and Being, turning paradigmatically *from* what immediately and always somewhat indeterminately shows itself, *to* that *eidos*, pure determinacy, that shines through it and empowers its showing, thus constituting its ground and its truth. Metaphysics will seldom, if at all, ask about what exceeds Being, about what would be *epekeina tēs ousias*, about the Dionysian abyss which exceeds metaphysics. In this respect, Nietzsche's text, broaching the abyss in the figure of Dionysus, exceeds metaphysics, transgresses it.

If the lines of the classical schema were still to be followed it would be necessary to consider next that Dionysian art in which the natural Dionysian state would be mimetically reproduced. Nietzsche is explicit about the schema: 'With reference to these immediate art-states of nature, every artist is an "imitator" . . . ' (§2). Dionysian art would arise as mimesis of the natural Dionysian state.

However, the lines of that classical schema are not simply to be followed, for the operation of Nietzsche's text, its excess, has begun to efface those lines. Consider, more importantly, how the operation of the concept of mimesis must be altered in a text which exceeds metaphysics. Or rather, consider first how the operation of the figure of mimesis is possible within the text of metaphysics.

Recall the founding text, Aristotle's *Poetics*. In that text, Aristotle sets out to discover the *eidos* of *poiētikē*, that is, he poses with respect to art the question that metaphysics will pose to every being, the question '*ti esti . . . ?*', the question as to what it is, the question as to what will later (through a certain transformation) be called its *essence*. The essence of art proves to be mimesis – and Aristotle's task becomes that of determining what this essence is, thus reiterating the essential question, posing the quetion of the essence of mimesis, the question of the essence of the essence of art. Thus mimesis would be doubly related to essence, constituting the essence of art and forming itself the object of a reiterated question of essence.

But how is this relation possible, this relation between mimesis and essence? Is not mimesis opposed to essence? Is not mimesis a doubling, unlimitable and uncontrollable, a scattering, a dispersal into unlimited multiplicity? Is it not precisely one of those operations which metaphysics would limit by opposing to it the Socratic turn to *logoi*, the gathering of manifoldness into the unity of an *eidos*, an essence? How then could mimesis be an essence, and how could there be an essence of mimesis? Such conjunctions would be possible only in so far as the figure of mimesis undergoes a certain reduction, a reduction by which is excluded, repressed, its opposition to essence, to metaphysical gathering. In the text of metaphysics – as the very condition of its belonging to the text of metaphysics – mimesis must be reduced to controllable imitation of beings, or, at best, imitation of the universal in a particular, of Being in a being. Art would, in its highest vocation, enter the circle between Being and beings, yet from the beginning it would be an inferior circling, and in a sense one could always have said what Hegel finally proclaimed as the end of art: 'Art is and remains for us, on the side of its highest vocation, something past.' Even for Aristotle mimesis is merely the way in which one learns during childhood, that is, under the control of others – for whom such means of learning is something past. Thus mimesis, an operation of unlimited dispersal, is domesticated, repressed, within the text of metaphysics, its figure both inverted and denatured so as to be superimposable upon the inferior portion of the linear figure of metaphysics.

However, Nietzsche's text, drawing the figure of Dionysus, exceeds metaphysics. The question is whether in this same transgression Nietzsche's text also frees mimesis from the repression to which it was subjected within metaphysics.

Let us return to Nietzsche's text, to the place in *The Birth of Tragedy* where Nietzsche conjoins nature and art, where he adds to the Dionysian state its artistic mimesis:

> In the first place, as a Dionysian artist he has become completely one with the proto-one [*mit dem Ur-Einen . . . eins geworden*], its grief and contradiction; and he produces the copy [*Abbild*] of this proto-one as music, assuming that music has been correctly termed a repetition [*Wiederholung*] and a recast [*ein zweiter Abguβ*] of the world (§5).

This invocation of the Dionysian artist requires the most careful consideration.

The passage could be – and nearly always has been – read as one of those points at which Nietzsche's text is most explicitly secured to metaphysics. The Dionysian state into which the Dionysian artist must already have entered would, on such a reading, be regarded as a matter of unification with the original, unitary will, the original *an sich*, of which everything else, including one's own phenomenal existence, is mere appearance. Music would then be an imitation of the will and tragedy the projection of such music upon the dramatic stage. Even in its highest form, as tragedy, art would merely circle within the circle of metaphysics, in this case within the circle, specifically, of Schopenhauerian metaphysics, that circle joining the one will to the many appearances. Nietzsche's text, thus secured, would become a metaphysical fable of the will, enforcing the metaphysical reduction of art. The figure of Dionysus, cut to the measure of the original *an sich*, the one will, would preserve no trace of transgression, and Nietzsche's text would in no wise exceed metaphysics toward the abyss.

And yet, much can be brought against such a reading – for example, Nietzsche's 'Attempt at a Self-Criticism' (1886), in which he voices his regret that he 'tried laboriously to express by means of Schopenhauerian and Kantian formulas strange and new valuations which fundamentally ran counter to the spirit of Kant and of Schopenhauer, as well as to their taste'.[3] And in *Ecce*

Homo Nietzsche is willing to consign only a few formulas to the Schopenhauerian circle: 'the cadaverous perfume of Schopenhauer clings only to a few formulas'.[4] But the withdrawal of *The Birth of Tragedy* from the Schopenhauerian circle is not only something retrospectively announced. Indeed, the entire fragmented discourse of *ekstasis*, which deposits traces throughout Nietzsche's text but which is voiced most openly in certain unpublished notes, runs utterly counter to the fragments of metaphysical discourse still intact in that text. The note that I have already cited, for example, or the following, dated winter 1869–spring 1870: All art demands a 'being-outside-oneself', an *ekstasis*; it is from this that drama proceeds, in so far as we in our *ekstasis* turn nothing back into ourselves but rather enter into an alien being.[5] Another note written between September 1870 and January 1871 is still more decisive: Representation is thus the birth of the will, and so multiplicity is already in the will.[6] The Schopenhauerian circle is here broken up quite decisively: the will is not simply *an sich*, in distinction from the appearances which arise through the activity of representation; and the will is not simply one, in distinction from the multiplicity of appearances. The disruption is more explicit yet in a note written probably in the mid-1880s as part of a draft for a preface to the new edition of *The Birth of Tragedy*: The antithesis of a real and an apparent world is lacking here: there is only *one* world.[7] The Dionysian is not *one* over against *many* but the exceeding of every such determinacy as would allow the delimitation of a one. The Dionysian is not *a* one but *the* one; or, more precisely, it is the oneness that issues not from determination but from the exceeding of all determination, that is, indeterminate – or, more precisely, indetermining – oneness.

The Dionysian artist must already have entered into the Dionysian state, into that ecstatic state of dissolution into the indetermining one; he must have become one with this proto-one in and as which all determinate ones, everything individual, undergoes indetermination. Thus the Dionysian artist must already have undergone a certain dissolution of his own individuality; and this is why Nietzsche insists that the individual is only a medium and not the genuine artistic creator. Contrary to the classical schema with which the metaphysical repression of art would be enforced, this means that it is not a matter of an individual artist adding art to nature, producing a mimetic double of the natural Dionysian state, but of nature adding art to itself, of mimetic excess being born from the very operation of what metaphysics would call excess *as such*, that is, the operation of the figure of Dionysus.

What is born from excess is, in the passage I have cited, at first quite provisionally designated as a copy (*Abbild*) of the proto-one, a repetition (*Wiederholung*). But the continuation of the passage makes it explicit that Dionysian repetition has nothing to do with images, much less with copies in any ordinary sense. It is rather, in Nietzsche's phrases, a matter of 'proto-reverberation' (*Urwiderklang*) or, still more significantly, and bordering on contradiction, 'imageless reflection' (*bildloser Wiederschein*). The Dionysian musician is, in Nietzsche's words, '*ohne jedes Bild*', and does not deal in images. Dionysian mimesis is then a reflection in which the Dionysian state somehow shines forth, announces itself, makes itself manifest, yet without its manifestation taking place through images. The figure of Dionysus announces itself in an imageless manifestation. Presumably this is why it must occur as music, assuming that music is the only art without images. And it is thus that, beyond Dionysian music, there is need that tragedy be born, that Apollonian images be made to reflect the image-less manifestation of the Dionysian.

Yet how is it that Dionysian mimesis is imageless? How is it that the figure of Dionysus withholds itself from the direct disclosure in an image? It is because, in both senses of the word, there is *nothing* to be disclosed – no being, no ground, not even Being (e.g., as *eidos*), but only the abyss of indetermination, nothing. Here it is a matter of mimesis of what would be *epekeina tēs ousias*, of the nothing that delimits Being; a matter of mimesis of what would be in excess of Being; a matter of mimesis freed from its metaphysical repression; a mimesis in excess of metaphysics.

Notes

1 *GT*, in *Werke: Kritische Gesamtausgabe*, ed. Colli & Montinari, Berlin, Walter de Gruyter, 1972, III, 1. References to this work will be given in the text by section number.
2 *Werke*, III, 3, p. 6

3 *Werke*, III, 1, p. 13
4 *Werke*, VI, 3, p. 308
5 *Werke*, III, 3, pp. 52f
6 *Werke*, III, 3, p. 118
7 *WM*, Stuttgart, Alfred Kröner Verlag, 1964, par. 853

· 2 ·

Heidegger
and the Nietzschean
'Physiology of Art'

MICHEL HAAR

'If there is to be art, if there is to be
any aesthetic doing and observing,
one physiological precondition is indispensable: rapture.'
NIETZSCHE

'When Nietzsche says 'physiology' doubtless he means
to emphasize the bodily state; but the bodily state
is in itself always already something psychical . . .
For Nietzsche, rapture means the most glorious victory of form.'
HEIDEGGER

The general tendency of Heidegger's interpretation of Nietzsche is apparently reductive. It consists in showing how Nietzschean philosophy remains imprisoned within the structures of traditional metaphysics; so that, for example, the Will to Power and the Eternal Return correspond to the metaphysical concepts of *essence* and *existence*; so that the traditional definition of truth as *adequatio, homoïôsis,* is never brought into question; so that the very essence of nihilism remains unthought; and so on. However, it would seem that there exists at the same time another tendency, which consists, in contrary fashion, of 'saving' Nietzsche from metaphysics, justifying him, as it were, by showing for example that his vocabulary betrays a more radically innovative intention or one which anticipates phenomenology.

It is surprising to note that this 'apology' for Nietzsche appears especially in the interpretation of Nietzsche's aesthetics. For example, Heidegger suggests that Nietzsche clears a path to a 'new interpretation of the sensible', one which might escape the Platonic dualism of the sensible and the supra-sensible. Heidegger also shows that the Nietzschean concept of *appearance*, which is not opposed either to essence or to reality, already moves in the phenomenological direction of a *shining forth*. Despite his doctrine of perspectivism, in which one still finds the relativistic Platonic notion of necessary illusion or error, Nietzsche values art so highly only because it makes manifest the *phenomenal* character of reality. Art makes the very *shining* of things apparent, and in so doing transfigures them. 'Art', writes Heidegger, 'induces reality, which is in itself a shining, to shine most profoundly and supremely in scintillating transfiguration.'[1] Neither of these two points is very extensively developed.

There is one point, however, on which Heidegger dwells at length and gives a large number of arguments, and that is the theme of the 'physiology of art'. That art might be the expression of a bodily state does not, in Heidegger's opinion, mean that Nietzsche sustains a biological or organicist interpretation of artistic creation and thus a deterministic one: What is strange and almost incomprehensible is the fact that he tries to make his conception of the aesthetic state accessible to his contemporaries, and tries to convince them of it, by speaking the language of physiology and biology.[2] Through a positivistic, materialistic language, Nietzsche would, in fact, have wanted to say just the opposite. There are two reasons for this. First, that in fact the life Nietzsche speaks of has nothing whatsoever to do with an object of scientific observation: it is the Will to Power's metaphysical essence. Secondly, and above all, that the bodily state described by Nietzsche as the condition both of artistic creation and of receptivity to art, the state he calls the fundamental aesthetic state, intoxication or rapture (*Rausch*), does not designate, despite the terms employed, a state of the physical, animal body (*Körper*). It means rather a *Stimmung* or affective disposition which is neither purely physical nor purely psychological, neither objective nor subjective. This *Stimmung* belongs to the 'lived body' (*Leib*), as it has been described by phenomenology. The question that arises from this is whether Heidegger doesn't go too far in his 'saving' of

Nietzsche. Is the distinction between *Körper* and *Leib* one that has meaning in Nietzsche? Doesn't Heidegger introduce the phenomenological meaning of the body into Nietzschean physiology somewhat obtrusively?

Why hide or attempt to minimize the dimensions of *facticity* which Nietzsche attributes to the body? Why should the body as an organism not have any role in the creative and receptive processes of art? Doesn't Heidegger really show here his embarrassment over the human body which, he says in the *Letter on Humanism*, is a close relative of the living being and yet separated from it by an *abyss*? When Nietzsche establishes a relationship between the artist's creative instinct and the diffusion of semen in the bloodstream,[3] or when he indicates that 'rapture' implies objective changes in the circulatory, nervous, and motor systems,[4] it does not seem very straightforward to attribute these clearly physiological indications to pure *Stimmung*! What are Heidegger's arguments in support of the notion of *Stimmung* and against physiology? Does not Nietzsche also criticise the purely physiological inasmuch as he rejects all determinism, every relationship of mechanistic causality between bodily states and art? On the other hand, is not Heidegger correct, in spite of his withdrawal from everything bodily, to show that intoxication or rapture is equivalent to a movement of transcendence in which the creator goes outside himself in order to unveil forms? Heidegger is right to show that intoxication in Nietzsche does not mean mental confusion, fuzziness, blindness or mere passivity, but is hyperlucid, clairvoyant, capable of 'seeing' the main features of Being and of revealing forms.

Yet here we touch the most sensitive point in Heidegger's interpretation, as it seeks to save Nietzsche not only from any 'physiologism' but also from any subjectivism. In a rather daring inversion of terms, Heidegger explains that it is not intoxication or rapture considered as a subjective state which is the necessary condition to the production of forms; rather, it is form or, if you prefer, beauty which awakens rapture in the subject. 'Beauty as an attuning thoroughly determines the state of man.'[5] Although he is not speaking here of beauty in itself, since 'beauty is not the object of a pure representation', it is the *eidos*, he says, in its original meaning of the face or aspect of what shows itself, which produces the extraordinary force of rapture. Rapture corresponds and responds to the unconcealment of Being. Thus rapture, writes Heidegger, 'explodes the very subjectivity of the subject . . . The aesthetic state is neither subjective nor objective.'[6] Here, Heidegger obviously tries to bring Nietzsche over to his own side, that is, to his conception of the work as the origin of art and of the work as the working out of truth itself, understood as self-manifestation of Being. 'The essence of the work', says Heidegger, 'is at the source of the essence of creation.'[7] The essence of truth as the self-manifestation of forms is in turn the origin of the essence of work. Isn't Heidegger wrongfully replacing here the Nietzschean primacy of *force* by a primacy of *form* that is based on his doctrine of *aletheia*? He acknowledges the fact that there is almost no consideration of form in Nietzsche, nor of the essence of form in relation to art; *'for that, he would have to take the work of art as his point of departure'*.[8]

Heidegger's aim, as he makes a shift from the Nietzschean doctrine of force to a doctrine of form, is clarified in his analysis of the notion of *chaos*. There too we will see that, for Heidegger, chaos is the 'pulsional' element, the multitude of elementary forces, but in no sense the un-ordered: chaos is 'that whose order is *hidden*, whose law is not immediately known to us'.[9] Isn't Heidegger closer to the Aristotelian notion of form immanent in nature than to the Nietzschean notion of nature as chaos? Doesn't the latter belong to an entirely different order from nature in the phenomenological sense (i.e. from the pure presence-at-hand), which is never the ground of things but is always reduced to a being appearing within the horizon of the world?

Rapture as Stimmung: *the Heideggerian interpretation of the body, and the criticism of physiology*

By interpreting intoxication or rapture as *Stimmung*, Heidegger means to reinstate Nietzsche's true thought on the body, a thought which he finds disfigured by a physiological and naturalistic terminology. In order to grasp Nietzsche's essential intention, one must have a viewpoint 'disengaged from everything unfortunate that Nietzsche shared with his time'.[10] The basic aesthetic state of rapture is not a purely bodily state, nor even a psychological, purely interior state, but an affective disposition in which Being in its totality reveals itself. This doctrine of *Stimmung* implies for Heidegger both *passivity* and *transcendence*: passivity, because a mood is an allowing oneself to be determined and disposed (*sich-Be-stimmen und Stimmen-lassen*) by Being; and transcendence, because by our moods we are lifted, transported, outside ourselves. Transcendence is thus submitted to passivity: 'every understanding is attuned'. As early as *Sein und Zeit* (§29), Heidegger emphasizes the passivity of *Dasein* with respect to *Stimmung*. '*Stimmung* takes hold of (*überfallt*) us. It comes neither from without nor from within; it springs from being-in-the-world itself.'[11] It is not a psychological state that projects itself outward, but a way of being in the world. We do not decide to be in such or such a frame of mind. If we rid ourselves of one state of mind or mood, another comes to take its place. It is *Stimmung* which determines whether we are affected, whether we have what Aristotle calls *pathemata tēs psychēs*, affections of the soul. *Stimmungen* mean that *Dasein* is receptive towards its own being-in-the-world. This receptiveness is not a determinism. To say that the bodily state is *Stimmung* means therefore that the body goes beyond itself towards the psychic, as it opens up to the world. 'The bodily state is, of itself, always already something psychical.'[12] This opening up is not voluntary and is not decided. With respect to Nietzsche's position, one wonders whether Heidegger does not minimize two important elements: 1. the activity (rapture, says Nietzsche, is a feeling of intensified force), and 2. the bodily, in the narrow sense of objective physiological states, that is to say, changes in the organism which are observable from without. Let us see what Heidegger's arguments against physiology are.

Heidegger rightly emphasizes the fact that when Nietzsche speaks of the body, he is not speaking of a part of the human being, but of the totality of man. 'The soul', says Nietzsche, 'is a name for a certain part of the body.' Consequently, it cannot be a matter of physiology in the scientific sense, as science necessarily studies a specific area of beings, but rather of 'physiology' in a *metaphysical* sense. It designates *physis*, or the artistic Will to Power.

His second argument is that the affective state which is rapture cannot be assimilated to natural processes as conceived by the positive sciences, for Nietzsche would then have to recognize the validity in themselves of the laws of nature and of the cause-effect relations.[13] But Nietzsche considers the laws and the relations of cause and effect as fictions.

Finally, Heidegger argues that positivist scientific physiology would preclude any decision, any selection, any instituting of values. In Nietzsche, he says, there is a choice in favour of art as a move against nihilism; Nietzsche is interested in promoting and cultivating art more than he is science. 'To define art at once as an anti-nihilistic movement and as the object of physiology is to try to mix fire with water.'[14] By water, Nietzsche understands the reactive, the determined; by fire the active, the affirmative. Moreover, if we stop at purely physiological variations in the body (blood content, temperature, secretions, etc.) we forget entirely the other aspect of the creative process, the fact of being 'lifted up or out beyond oneself',[15] in other words, transcendence, which, says Heidegger, is, of course, something very different from a mere 'aspect' of *Dasein* among others. All these arguments come back to a single one: there is no 'pure' physiology, except for science, and a short-sighted science at that. Outside of it, physiology refers us back to metaphysics: to the will or to transcendence.

For Heidegger, to think of the biological as such as to think of nothing at all. But for him, it is only a short step from this to saying that there is no physiology, and denying not only objectivity but also facticity, a step which Heidegger takes when he reduces Nietzsche's *intensification of strength* – in rapture – to the mere intensified *feeling of strength*. 'The intensifiation does not imply here', he insists, 'that an "objective" increase, or a superabundance of strength, comes into play; it should be understood in relation to the *Stimmung*.'[16] Does Heidegger not lean somewhat towards idealism in this? In repudiating the body as an organism, does he not repudiate the body itself? Does the body have an ontological status of its own in Heidegger's philosophy? This last question would carry us far afield. Suffice it here to recall that for Heidegger, man as being-there, *Dasein*, eksistent, open to being, does not need to have or to be a body in order to be understood or defined. 'The body, our being embodied (*das Leiben*), says Heidegger, is something *essentially other* than the simple fact of being encumbered with an organism.'[17] Apart from this, Heidegger gives almost nothing but negative definitions of the human body; he insists that it is radically different from a living organism, separated from it by a gulf, not the same as *Vorhandenheit* or the present-at-hand, or the *Körper*, the physical body. Positively speaking, the body is inseparable from the *Stimmung*; thanks to it, 'the body in its bodily states permeates the self'.[18] It is *Stimmung* 'which determines beforehand the implicative investment of the body in our *Dasein*' (*einbehaltender Einbezug des Leibes im Dasein*).[19] 'Feeling as the fact of *self-feeling* constitutes precisely the way in which we are bodily.'[20] Now feeling, *Gefühl* or *Stimmung*, is transcendence: '*Stimmung* is precisely the fundamental way in which we are *outside* of ourselves.'[21] In defining the body as ecstatic openness, Heidegger seems to turn his back on any factuality of the body.

To counter this leap into transcendence – rapture reduced to a self-surpassing state – we may recall not only Nietzsche's description of concrete bodily states but also his constant affirming that 'aesthetics is nothing other than an applied physiology', that 'aesthetics has no meaning if it is not a science of nature',[22] that aesthetic values are only biological feelings of well-being. Heidegger's only argument to refute all this is that by biology Nietzsche did not mean a science, but life as Will to Power. Nevertheless, a re-reading of Nietzsche's texts on artistic bodily states would suggest another intermediate path between the science that Nietzsche is the first to deny and the abstractedness of a purely transcendental position that tends to idealize the body.

The body as artist

In his reading of the physiology of art, Heidegger leaves aside, as we have seen, several conditions of fact regarding the making and the receiving of art, conditions hardly assimilable to *Stimmung*, that is, to a pure transcendence without reference to a bodily state. When Heidegger does allude – and with embarrassment – to inescapably biological conditions such as intensified bodily strength, pleasure, sensuality, animal well-being, or, more rarely, malaise, he always attempts to bring them back to the psychic, or else to show that they must be 'restrained, overcome and surpassed'.[23] On the other hand, he does not ever mention states relative to sexuality, whether sublimated or not, to cruelty, or to psychopathology (neurosis or madness, particularly Dionysian madness). We shall examine these traits before we formulate any objections to this Heideggerian interpretation or absence of interpretation.

For Nietzsche, art is an *intensification of physical strength*. Rapture means an 'increase' in objective strength, both in the creator and in the receiver. There can be no doubt about this: 'strength, the sensation of muscular sovereignty, of suppleness and pleasure in movement, of dance, of lightness, of vivacity, the strength which is the pleasure of showing one's strength.'[24] And again:

All kinds of art act suggestively on the muscles and the senses, which are active from the first in a man who is naïvely artistic; art never speaks to any but artists – it speaks to their kind of more subtle bodily flexibility . . . All art works *tonically*, increases strength . . . one hears with one's muscles, one even reads with the muscles.[25]

Responding 'before the fact' to Heidegger's interpretation, as it were, Nietzsche does indicate that this overabundance of strength (which is created, for example, by the rapture of being in love, a naïvely artistic state) is not illusory, but a real increase.

Art does more than merely imagine; it even transposes values. And it is not only that it transposes the *feeling of values*; the lover *is* more valuable is stronger. In animals, this condition produces new weapons, pigments, colours, and forms; above all, new movements, new rhythms, new love-calls and seductions. It is no different with man.[26]

This superabundance of strength can be felt as a painful tension which must be eased: 'One must first think of this condition as a compulsion and urge to get rid of the exuberance of inner tension through muscular activity and movements of all kinds.'[27] But most often, the superabundance of strength is accompanied by a feeling of pleasure.

It is surprising to notice that Heidegger does not devote a single analysis to art as pleasure, as 'sensual feast', whether it be the pleasure of the receiver or that which leads to creation. In the first version of *The Origin of the Artwork*, the unpublished lecture of 1935, he even rejects *Genuss*, enjoyment, as an authentic relation to art; he calls it *Erhitzung*, getting excited, getting hot.

If rapture is only another name for pleasure ('the pleasurable state which is known as rapture'[28]), what does Nietzsche mean by the word *pleasure*?

Sometimes he uses it in the larger sense of joy, gladness-to-be-alive, which implies a certain spirituality, a transfiguring vision.

> The states in which we infuse a transfiguration and fullness and joy in life: sexuality, intoxication, feasting, spring, victory over an enemy, mockery, bravado, cruelty, the ecstasy of religious feeling. Three elements principally: sexuality, rapture, cruelty – all belong to the oldest festal joys of mankind, all equally preponderate in the early 'artist'.[29]

Let us note that sexuality comes first, even before rapture. We shall return to this in a moment. But most often, by pleasure Nietzsche means the *pleasure of the senses*, which depends on a stimulation (*Reiz*) of the corresponding bodily zones.

> Conversely, when we encounter things that display this transfiguration and fullness, the animal existence (*Dasein*) responds with an excitation of those spheres in which all those pleasurable states are situated – and a blending of those very delicate nuances of animal well-being and desires constitutes the *aesthetic state*.[30]

In this case, the aesthetic state is evidently associated with an overflowing vitality and with bodily health in a biological, even medical sense of the word.

> Art reminds us of states of animal vigor; it is on the one hand an excess and overflow of blossoming physicality into the world of images and desires; on the other, an excitation of the animal functions through the images and desires of intensified life; an enhancement of the feeling of life, a stimulant to it.[31]

Nietzsche goes so far as to associate with physical pleasure and animal well-being the satisfaction taken in order and logic. 'Pleasure in the orderly, in what can be grasped as a whole, in what is defined within limits, in repetition, this pleasure belongs to the feelings of well-being of all organic beings.'[32] Very often indeed Nietzsche marks the analogy between physical and logical pleasure, but he establishes a derivative relation in the following way: *physical* pleasure becomes *logical* pleasure, which becomes *aesthetic* pleasure. 'Logical and geometrical simplification in a consequence of enhancement of strength.'[32] And again, 'The feeling of logical and geometrical satisfaction constitutes the *basis* of aesthetic evaluations.'[33] Thus the pleasure of the senses and of the healthy body, which art celebrates, very clearly constitutes the ground of more spiritual values (logical, aesthetic values). If all art is first the extension of a state of physical well-being, we can understand how art in general can be a blessing, an affirmation of existence. 'Art is essentially affirmation, blessing, divinisation of existence.'[34] To speak of pessimistic art is a contradiction; 'by saying that something is "beautiful", we affirm it'.[35]

But then, how does Nietzsche explain that certain works of art are complacent in the representation of ugliness or of the unhealthy? He himself takes Zola as an example of this, and also Dostoyevski. Yet for Nietzsche, there is no ugliness in art. The ugly exists only in reality. It is the contrary of art. The ugly is powerlessness to create because of the impoverishment of life.[36] The ugly is always transfigured in art. Art means that a superior force has been able to master even the ugly.

> The representation of things which are dreadful and disquieting is itself in the artist an instinct for power and splendour, and is possible because he does not fear them . . . Zola? . . . the Goncourt brothers? The things they show are ugly, but they show them because they take pleasure in their ugliness.[37]

The interpretation of the ugly concords with Nietzsche's famous interpretation of the tragic as a symptom of increased strength. 'The predilection for all that is ambiguous and fearful is a sign of strength. A taste for tragedy characterized strong ages and temperaments.'[38]

This little detour around the question of the ugly may clarify for us the overall meaning of pleasure for Nietzsche. First, pleasure as such is not sought after, is not an end in itself. 'It is not true that man seeks pleasure . . . what man wants is an increase of power.'[39] That which is pursued is the greater force. Heidegger is right on this point. Pleasure is the corollary of the affirmative Will to Power. 'The will for more is inherent in the essence of pleasure; it wants increase of power.'[40] Second, pleasure does not exclude pain; on the contrary, inasmuch as the Will to Power seeks resistance, obstacles to overcome, pain to confront. Nietzsche goes so far – and this is something that reminds us of the Leibnizian theodicy – as to say that the world – if all its pain were eliminated – would be unaesthetic.[41] Nietzsche is opposed to all eudemonism, to all those who in weariness aspire to happiness as to 'the sabbath of sabbaths'. In spite of this *ontological* character of pleasure, as a corollary accompaniment of the Will to Power ('every increase of power is pleasure'),[42] it is impossible to get rid of the organic, physical dimension. To dissociate strength as Will to Power from bodily dispositions is to make the latter into mere emanations or surface traits of the essence that Will to Power is, and to posit Being (*Sein*) separately from beings (*Seienden*) – which Nietzsche does not do.

Art does not eliminate physiology, but rather makes it intelligent; as Nietzsche says in French in the text: 'art is an *intelligente* sensuality'.[43] This is the point on which I would criticise Heidegger, who speaks of a 'reversal' (*Umschlag*)[44] by which the physiological becomes that which must be completely reabsorbed. 'Bodily conditions', says Heidegger, 'turn out to be all that we must tame, vanquish, resolve into the created work.'[45] Here Heidegger attributes an exaggerated degree of importance to the notion of form, of rule, basing his interpretation on a single passage in Nietzsche. 'One is an artist at the cost of experiencing that which all non-artists call "form" as *content*, as the "thing itself".[46] Physiological dispositions remain as the very atmosphere of creation as well as of aesthetic enjoyment, even among the classical artists whom Nietzsche so admires. There is a sort of asceticism or puritanism in Heidegger, while Nietzsche speaks of the pleasure of the classicists in keeping to proportion, in spite of a strong sensuality (which by that very fact is not eliminated, but conserved): 'the pleasure aesthetic natures naturally take in proportion; the enjoyment that beauty affords them'.[47] In a very important fragment on classical style, Nietzsche insists on the fact that in Apollonian rapture, 'sexuality and voluptuous pleasure are not absent' but are 'quieted, simplified, concentrated, abbreviated'.[48] Heidegger retains nothing of this except the powerful stylisation of what Nietzsche calls the *grand style*, forgetting, meanwhile, that it constitutes a double pleasure: the state of enjoyment (based in the body) is conserved and reinforced by its concentration. That excitement and excitability be mastered does not mean that they are diminished or reabsorbed; on the contrary, they are heightened.

Heidegger's puritanism is still more striking where sexuality is concerned.[49] To be fair, while his assertions on the sexual conditions of artistic creation are repeated and vigorous, Nietzsche nevertheless maintains a theory of necessary sublimation which resembles somewhat Freud's doctrine. Schematically stated, it says that artists are individuals whose sexuality is both strong and controlled. First of all Nietzsche posits that sexuality and affirmative strength are one single thing: 'It is the same strength that is spent in the sex act as in artistic creation. There is only one kind of strength.'[50] 'Raphael would be incomprehensible without a certain overheating of his sexual self. To make music is another way of making children.'[51] 'Sexual rapture is the oldest and most orignal kind.' Numerous fragments[52] mention overabundant sex drives as the first condition of rapture in general, and especially Dionysian rapture. But the powerful sexuality of artists is controlled at once by calculation and by instinct. 'The artist is perhaps necessarily a sensual man . . . But in the acting out of his mission, of his will to achieve mastery, *he is generally temperate, even chaste*. His dominant instinct forces him to be so.'[53] In the same way, there is a sublimated satisfaction on the part of the spectator: 'The demand for art and for beauty is an indirect requirement for the raptures of sex drive.'[54]

The similar silence with which Heidegger treats mental imbalance, neurosis or psychosis, is also puzzling. Doubtless, Heidegger is to some extent justified in considering psychiatric classifications and vocabulary, as superficial and inappropriate for the phenomena to which he is referring. And yet Nietzsche devotes long passages to the relationship between art and madness. The connection is made in *The Birth of Tragedy*, for example, in which the Dionysian, in accord with an ancient tradition, is presented as madness; it is also made in the 'Attempt at a Self-Criticism' (1886, §4), where Nietzsche asks, 'what is, *physiologically speaking*, the meaning of this madness?' And he even recalls the famous passages in *Phaedrus* on the 'divine madness' of poetic inspiration. Nor does Heidegger say anything of Nietzsche's valuing of morbid states ('One cannot be an artist without being sick.'[55]), or of the analysis of the 'Greek neurosis' the famous 'neurosis of health', born of a superabundance of strength, which brought the Greeks to seek out the disquieting and sinister aspects of existence – not out of weakness, but in strength. Nietzsche opposes this neurosis of health to the pessimistic neurosis of certain nineteenth century artists, the Romantics, the Naturalists, the post-Romantics such as Wagner, whose neurotic art is addressed to neurotics in order to accentuate their malady and plunge them into states of hypnotic stupor. It is strange that Heidegger, who agrees with Nietzsche's pejorative diagnosis of Wagner, does not analyse the physio-psychological reasons linked to the general concept of 'neurosis' and sickness.

More generally speaking, should we simply reject and declare false the empirical, clinical, aspects of Nietzsche's physiological descriptions, because they are on an 'ontic' level and closely linked to the metaphysical ground of the Will to Power? Nietzsche's physiology is certainly not scientific, but it is perhaps not purely metaphysical, because it is also simply descriptive, quasi-phenomenological.

Chaos, forms and forces

In his analysis of rapture, Heidegger returns again and again to the essential link between rapture and the perception of forms. Rapture is not drunkenness, of course, nor is it a vague sense of well-being, or uncontrolled excitement, but rather a lucid vision of *forms*. Rapture means the most glorious victory of form.[56] Nietzsche shows in fact (and Heidegger does well to emphasize it) that artists see things not as they are but with greater force and simplicity, *according to their principal features*, and it is this that we superficially call artistic idealization. But the point at which Heidegger completely departs from the Nietzschean position is his claim that forms are simply encountered by the artist and revealed by him. 'The artist's vision *discerns* the simpler and stronger aspects in what he meets.'[57] But Nietzsche says that rapture *imposes* forms upon things through a kind of constraint: the artist does violence to nature. Never in Nietzsche does the artist submit to the structures of Being; instead he brings them forth. But Heidegger's most marked excess is deriving the artistic *Stimmung* from forms which would seem to exist prior to his creative work. Let us examine the passage that is, in my opinion, most obviously to be contested:

'Form defines and demarcates for the first time the realm in which the state of growing force and plenitude of being comes to fulfillment. Form founds the realm in which rapture as such becomes possible. Wherever form holds sway, as the supreme simplicity of the most resourceful lawfulness, there is rapture.'[58]

As Heidegger says further on, neither the aesthetic state, nor the creative act can be the 'determining element', but only form.[59]

In giving precedence to form in this way, whereas in the notion of the 'grand style' Nietzsche rather speaks precisely of rule or law, Heidegger purposely underestimates the importance of force. Form is only a temporary guise or visage of the ever-changing strife of forces. Forms are fictions, useful creations that serve like values to uphold momentarily one bundle of forces or another. Form is a momentary point of equilibrium at which the expansion of a force has paused. Creation for Nietzsche, as *Schöpfung*, consists of dipping down into a reservoir of forces, not of forms. Forms are always surfaces and masks. Nietzsche is constantly returning from forms under their two essential aspects, images and rhythms, to the two artistic drives (Apollonian and Dionysian) from which they directly flow. Nietzsche's genealogy always comes back from forms to the forces – whether ascending or declining – that establish them.

If the body of the artist is at the core of creation, it is because through it and beyond it, the artist draws from the great body of universal life that Nietzsche calls, perhaps awkwardly, *chaos*. For the individual body is not the ultimate source of artistic activity, and thus is not its base. In this sense, Nietzsche is at the limits of aesthetics, in its traditional sense; perhaps he explodes it, for the subjective state of creator or spectator is not the final instance to which we can refer. As in *The Birth of Tragedy*, the last Nietzsche affirms that there are pre- and trans-individual artistic forces. Individuals are not isolated. 'There is a *common stream* that flows through all individuals.'[60] This 'common stream' is the Will to Power, which is not a metaphysical substance (as is, for example, in Schopenhauer, the will-to-live) but an element that presents itself originally to itself as chaos, that is, as an infinite play of forces dispersed in a multitude of perspectives and yet as a living universal medium common to all beings. Perhaps it is difficult to understand how the infinite difference, which is the Will to Power as chaos, can be also the infinite unity of the vital flux. However we might manage, we can *not* understand the body without this reference to chaos. In itself, the body is multiplicity and unity; but above all it is an opening onto the great chaos of the world, or of nature, or of universal life. The body is not something isolated. Through it flows universal life, of which we receive only the faintest and most fleeting sparks. Heidegger says very justly that the body is only a 'cut-out' in the flux of chaos. 'Our living body billows like a wave in the flow of chaos'.[61]

Here once more, as he does apropos of rapture, Heidegger emphasizes strongly the fact that chaos is not confusion, a savage flowing together of sensations. 'Nietzsche does not mean by chaos the confused or the un-ordered, but the pulsional, forward-flowing, moving element whose order is hidden, whose law is not immediately known to us.'[62] Here again, Heidegger introduces – apparently against Nietzsche's deeper intention – the primacy of forms. For Nietzsche, there is not an order in and of itself of forms latent in chaos, but only one of forces, of intensities. Further, Heidegger shows his embarrassment in presenting chaos sometimes as a hidden order, or the secretly ordered current of universal life (is he referring here to the pre-Socratic *physis*?), sometimes as a fantastic projection of human subjectivity which would enlarge the image of the body to the dimensions of the universe. However, Nietzsche says in paragraph 109 of *The Gay Science* that chaos is not even the absence of beauty or of order, that one should beware of applying our human categories to the world, or of thinking of the universe as a great, living organism.

This interpretation of chaos as a hidden reservoir of forms limits, I think, the thrust of Heidegger's interpretation of art in Nietzsche as a return to chaos. Indeed, art is the risk of affronting chaos. The artist alone can bear to look upon chaos. 'I tell you, you must yet have chaos in you if you are to give birth to a dancing star. I tell you, you still have chaos in you.' (Prologue of *Zarathustra*). But chaos is rather on the side of what Heidegger calls the earth, the ground, or what Merleau-Ponty calls the pre-objective, or, in Nietzschean terms, the indeterminate surfeit of forces. Forms already belong to a constituted historical world: form is not *Ursprung*, not a primordial resource. If art imitates nature it is not nature as a reservoir of forms, an external model to be represented, but as obedience to forces and principally to the *Verstellungskraft*, the force which displaces forms, which pushes them into or out of the visible, into and out of presence. 'Art', says Heidegger, 'dares to risk chaos'. How could there be any risk, if the superabundance were only the wealth of forms hidden and waiting to be discovered? What is this risk? The risk is that art might end up being contrary to the grand style, might end up as an art in which the superabundance is not subjected to a form or a law, as a decadent, romantic, reactive art, like Wagnerian art as seen by Nietzsche. Hence it is finally force, the type of force, which decides. What matters to Nietzsche in art is not the *Gestalt*, it is the genesis of forms, the *Gestaltung*: Will to Power is defined as *die gestaltende Kraft*, 'the form-creating force'.

By conducting the aesthetic experience back to *Stimmung* and to its transcendence, Heidegger reveals the extent of his distrust with regard to nature, a distrust whose deep motives and consequences would deserve a thorough study.[63] He means to exclude the possibility that the body as a living being might possess any dynamic inventiveness worthy of being called artistic. Most of his demonstrations are denials: it is not the body that produces the Beautiful; it is not nature that inspires art.

Now, for Nietzsche, art is a name for a dimension of *physis*. 'Art itself wells up in man as a force of nature and disposes of him, whether he wills it or not.'[64] In strange affinity with Schelling, Nietzschean art derives originally from nature and not from human subjectivity. 'Artistic pleasure must', writes the young Nietzsche, 'exist as well primarily outside of men.'[65] Through physiology, art finds itself re-situated in the non-totalizable totality of natural energies. Artistic production does not, in the last analysis, derive from a calculation of the intellect and of a conscious will, although the artist is perfectly capable of it. It is an unmasterable *physis* which plays and comes to light through the artist's gestures. That this *physis* be thought as Will to Power does not invalidate but rather confirms the phenomenological truth of a creative spontaneity of the body. Without this unmasterable artist's *physis*, all art works would be reducible to the illustration of ideas by images and rhythms.

Every artist knows well, even when he or she ventures constructing doctrines about so-called 'creative thought', that the work of the body, the gestures of the hands, is dictated by a necessity and an authority both younger and more ancient than the artist. Let us leave the last word on the question to Nietzsche:

Even in our time, namely in artists, one finds in abundance a sort of wonder, a respectful way of leaving the answer in suspense, when they are asked to question how they performed their master stroke (*der beste*

Wurf) and from what sphere the creative thought came to them: they feel, when they ask themselves this question, a sort of innocence or childlike modesty; hardly do they dare to say, 'It came out of me, it was my hand that threw the dice.'[66]

Notes

1 Martin Heidegger, *Nietzsche*, vol. I, Neske, Pfullingen, 1961, p.249; Martin Heidegger, *The Will to Power as Art*, translated by David Farrell Krell, New York, Harper and Row, 1979, p.216. Hereafter these will be cited as *NI* and *WPA* respectively.
2 *WPA*, p.113
3 *WM*, §805
4 Ibid., §807
5 *WPA*, p.123
6 Ibid., p.123
7 Ibid., p.115
8 Ibid., p.120
9 *NI*, p.566
10 *WPA*, p.127
11 *Sein und Zeit*, Tubingen, Max Niemeyer, 1979, p.136
12 *WPA*, p.96
13 Ibid., p.93
14 Ibid., p.93
15 Ibid., p.116
16 Ibid., p.100 (translation mine)
17 Ibid., p.99
18 Ibid., p.98
19 Ibid., p.99 (translation mine)
20 Ibid., p.98
21 Ibid., p.99
22 *Grossoktav Ausgabe*, Leipzig, Kröner, 1917, IX, p.286 (par.2), 1 hereafter *GA*
23 *WPA*, p.129
24 *WM*, §800
25 Ibid., §809
26 Ibid., §808
27 Ibid., §811
28 Ibid., §800
29 Ibid., §801
30 Ibid., §801
31 Ibid., §802
32 *Werke: Kritische Gesamtausgabe*, ed. Colli & Montinari, Berlin,

Walter de Gruyter, 1973, VII, 3, p.35. See also Ibid., p.34. This edition hereafter cited as *Werke*.

33 *Werke*, VII, 3, p.35

34 *WM*, §821

35 Ibid., §852

36 Ibid., §809

37 Ibid., §821

38 Ibid., §852

39 Ibid., §702

40 Ibid., §695

41 *GA*, Kröner, XIII, §227

42 *WM*, §693. See also Ibid., §702

43 Ibid., §800

44 *NI*, p.152

45 Ibid., p.152

46 *WM*, §818

47 Ibid., §870

48 *WM*, §799

49 The ontological interpretation of sexuality (*Geschlechtichkeit*) in volume 26 of the *Gesamtausgabe* (*The Metaphysical Principles of Logic* §10) and the factual dispersion (*Zerstreuung*) into two sexes of the originally 'neuter' *Dasein* would require a lengthy special analysis. See J. Derrida, 'Geschlecht', in *Martin Heidegger*, ed. Michel Haar, Paris, Cahiers de L'Herne, 1983.

50 *WM*, §815

51 Ibid., §800

52 See *WM*, §800; 801; 804; 805; 806; 807; 808

53 Ibid., §813

54 Ibid., §805, my italicization of *indirect*

55 Ibid., §811

56 *WPA*, p.119

57 Ibid., p.118, my italics for *discerns*, *heraussieht* (translation mine)

58 Ibid., p.119

59 *NI*, p.162

60 *WM*, §686

61 *NI*, p.569

62 Ibid., p.566

63 See my book, *Le Chant de la Terre*, Paris, L'Herne, 1987

64 *WM*, §798

65 *Werke*, III, 3, 7. See Ibid., 16

66 *WM*, §659; *Werke*, VII, 3, 36 (36)

· 3 ·

Nietzsche's Transvaluation of Time

DAVID WOOD

For anyone who thinks that the radical rethinking of time and the temporal might turn to deconstructive strategies for assistance it must come as something of a shock to discover that deconstruction's most celebrated practitioner denies the possibility of a post-metaphysical theory of time, and indeed claims that Time itself is a metaphysical concept.[1] However, considering the extent to which the framework of Derrida's work is anticipated by Nietzsche, it is something of a challenge to try to understand Nietzsche's thought of eternal recurrence in the light of these strictures. Has Nietzsche managed to achieve by an indirect route what could not be brought about by a direct assault on the citadel? Nietzsche does not say all that much about Time *per se*, and yet his most fundamental concept – that of eternal recurrence – is an essentially temporal one.[2] I shall argue that, despite the persistence of the link between the temporal and the ontological which is so clear in Hegel, Husserl and Heidegger, Nietzsche does not, for all that, repeat the metaphysical motif of presence but subverts it instead. The account of the *moment* which Nietzsche offers us is fundamentally at odds with any such value as presence. I make the following more detailed claims:

1 Nietzsche offers us a brilliant example of how to displace a frame of reference from within. In this case it is that of the ordinary 'metaphysical' concept of time.

2 He retains the centrality of the instant only to explode the traditional value of such a primitive concept. With Nietzsche,

the instant opens onto what is other.

3 The instant is not merely a non-recuperative opening out, it is also an embodiment of all those identical moments it repeats. This 'repetition' could be said to be a most primitive kind of 'representation'.

4 If that is the case, Nietzsche's 'moment of intensity' builds representation into its most primitive 'element', which is thereby primitively not self-contained. (Connections with Derrida's 'trace' structure should be evident here.)

Broadly speaking, I treat Nietzsche's account as a reflective intensification of our understanding of the 'present', one which successfully subverts our everyday recuperative understanding. As such it belongs to the deconstructive phase of the rethinking of time, which, as I show elsewhere, is not the end of the story.[3]

Nietzsche radically questions, subverts and displaces 'our ordinary concept of time', at a number of different levels. Eternal recurrence, as they say, is an undecidable term, and I shall use this suggestion as a way of clarifying the various otherwise incompatible ways in which he explains it.

How, we might ask, is it in principle possible to avoid Derrida's strictures? Derrida, after all, admits that it is not concepts themselves which are or are not metaphysical, but their textual exploitation and functioning. This opens the way, I argue, to Nietzsche's use of such concepts. It may be, if we stick to some rather narrow sense of the term, that Nietzsche has not produced a new *concept* of time, but that he has replaced its status as a concept with something else. The impossibility of conceptualizing eternal recurrence may turn out to be a positive feature.

It is, however, worth asking ourselves initially whether we can properly talk about 'our ordinary concept of time'. This phrase can itself be understood in a common-sense way as our taken-for-granted understanding of time, but as St Augustine showed long ago, the attempt to transform this tacit understanding into something more conceptually rigorous is somewhat problematic. The other way of understanding the phrase would then rest on some such view (shared by Heidegger and Derrida) as that the one ordinary concept of time we all share is that derived from Aristotle. But are there not difficulties attached to the idea? Who are 'we'? Is it to be taken for granted that we all share a common concept of time? Might there not be a hidden complicity between the idea of a concept and some particular interpretation of time? Do we suppose there is but *one* concept of time? Let me develop this last question.

Far more 'ordinary' than having a unitary concept of time is the fact that we distinguish between different kinds of time: subjective/objective, existential/cosmic, qualitative/quantitative, time as experienced/time as measured, and so on. But what if each of these oppositions merely *distributed* according to an unanalysed schema (such as inside/outside) the same fundamental value (such as presence)? What if such a distribution functioned to *preserve* that value? It could be argued, for example, that the distinction between subjective and objective time is a conceptual labour that assures under each heading the preservation of the unity of the temporal series, and that this is achieved precisely by making this distinction. All events can then be *located* in one or other category by distinct rules of integration (such as narrativity for subjective time, seriality for objective time).

On such an argument, the fundamental unity of time would have been preserved precisely by multiplying the frames of reference within which it operates. Undoubtedly one then needs a further story to integrate these multiple frames. The usual one, with only two frames, is a story of derivation. Objective time is shown to be dependent on, derivative from subjective temporality, or vice versa. The point of my remarks here is to suggest that talk about 'our ordinary concept of time' in the singular need not be undermined by the fact that everywhere we find a duality or even plurality of such concepts. But it might make sense to allow that there *are* different ordinary concepts of time, and fall back on a more fundamental claim – that they each embody a basic set of common values, which we could call 'unity', 'integration', 'identity', or even more fundamentally, that of 'presence' as the condition of such values being realised. On Nietzsche's account these would be the values pertaining to Being. The traditional betrayal of time would consist in subjugating the values associated with Becoming to those of Being.

Nietzsche, Heidegger and Derrida share the view (and they are not alone) that the ordinary concept(s) of time embodies values which are more ontological than temporal. But in each case the lesson this insight teaches is that questions about time and questions about Being collapse into one another and cannot be separated, as Plato long ago made so apparent.

Each of them is also engaged not merely in a *critique* of the ordinary concept of time, but in what we might call, borrowing from Nietzsche, a *transvaluation* of time. And for Nietzsche especially, this is presented as the key to a human transformation, indeed a transformation which would point beyond 'man'. The focus of this transformative projection is the thought of eternal recurrence, announced in *The Gay Science*, claimed (in *Ecce Homo*) to be 'the fundamental conception' behind *Thus Spoke Zarathustra*, and the title of a projected book bequeathed to us in his *Nachlass*. One could avoid the analytical task of separating the various versions by saying that the thought of eternal recurrence is not a single thought at all, but a *constellation* or *family* of 'thoughts'. But this would only be a temporary, because largely uninformative, way of legitimating the diverse and seemingly contradictory accounts Nietzsche offers. Moreover, there are other considerations:

1 Nietzsche's mode of discourse and style of presentation vary from one account to another, making a comparison of the abstract 'thesis' in each case problematic. How, for example, should we compare the 'poetic' versions (there are a number in *Thus Spoke Zarathustra*[4]) and the scientific proofs in *The Will to Power*.[5]

2 The *rhetorical strategy* varies, and may indeed be the subject of critical disagreement. Again, that there was a 'content' to be drawn out for comparison would be made questionable in principle.

3 The audience/level of exposition varies. Would we necessarily expect esoteric and exoteric versions to be consistent?[6]

One can make a virtue out of contradiction (*vide* Walt Whitman, for whom contradiction was a sign of spiritual abundance). Jaspers' reading of Nietzsche does just this. Or one can offer general arguments drawing on the thesis of semantic indeterminacy or of the fictionality of truth and hence of consistency (both of which Nietzsche held). But these are mere slogans, signposts, the husks of thought; they are not in themselves arguments. And to sift through Nietzsche's various presentations of eternal recurrence for a discriminatory classification of the various accounts is essential. This will not be theoretically disinterested, but where these interests coincide with Nietzsche's, the reading can be productive. My own theoretical interest, to make it explicit, is in understanding the role of eternal recurrence in Nietzsche's transvaluation of time. The value of such a guiding interest remains to be seen. It is also an open question whether it can be sustained as such, as a 'theoretical interest', or whether the cool analytical security that such a phrase suggests is not itself fundamentally at risk. Placing what Nietzsche called the 'greatest weight' on the scales is not an act free from danger. Nonetheless I shall begin by arguing (a) that the various ways in which eternal recurrence is formulated reflect the different modes (levels, dimensions) at which time needs to be transvalued or 'deconstructed';[7] (b) that the question of the *status* of eternal recurrence (whether it is a concept, a theory, a thought, an experience, an ecstasy, a test . . .) will vary with the level in question above; (c) that we ought to take seriously the suggestion that eternal recurrence is 'undecidable' in terms of the conceptual framework it subverts. (What that implies is that not only would eternal recurrence be a 'moral' test [Try to affirm that!] but an intellectual test [Try to think that through!].)

To give some structure to this account I propose to distinguish three levels or ways in which eternal recurrence is presented: (a) cosmological, (b) psychological, and (c) ontological. It might be objected that this framework is not complete (what about the historical, for instance?), but perhaps it is not altogether 'naïve'. Of course, Nietzsche might put these very distinctions in question, but in my view the different presentations of eternal recurrence do work within such traditional categories, *if only to dissolve them.* And these categories also correspond to three different dimensions of time: (i) universal (including historical) time, (ii) what I will call 'motivational' time, (iii) time as linked with identity (both of things and persons). If the ordinary schemas and concepts of time can be understood to rest on the value of *unity* – guaranteeing it, reappropriating it, making it possible, etc. – then the deconstruction or transvaluation of time will invert and displace this value as it is specifically embodied in each mode, level or dimension.

Thus we find corresponding to the category of universal time the idea that time stretches infinitely in both directions, that it is one-dimensional, and that every event has a uniquely determined place within it. Ordinary motivational time can be glossed as a structure of asymmetry between past and future, in which the past is complete and unaffectable and the future the scene for the projection of one's freely chosen ends. Time understood ontologically, in relation to identity, is understood either as a neutral container in which things or persons endure as they are (substances), where their identity is independent of time, or as productive of identity by making possible the development of a being's identity to fulfilment or completion.

It is a sign of the polysemic depth of the idea of eternal recurrence that it works to transvalue each of these settings. Let us now look at some of Nietzsche's remarks that would bear out this reading. We shall turn first to the cosmological version of eternal recurrence.

The cosmological version

This is most explicitly formulated in *The Will to Powr* Nos. 1062 and 1066, and in various notes dating from 1885–8.[8] Let me quote, as countless others have done, Nietzsche's 'most scientific' argument for eternal recurrence:

> If the world may be thought of as a certain definite quantity of force and as a certain definite number of centres of force – and every other representation remains indefinite and therefore useless – it follows that, in the great dice game of existence, it must pass through a calculable number of combinations. In infinite time, every possible combination would at some time or another be realised; more: it would be realised an infinite number of times. And since between every combination and its next recurrence all other possible combinations would have to take place, and each of these combinations conditions the entire sequence of combinations in the same series, a circular movement that has already repeated itself infinitely often and plays its game in infinitum.[9]

We begin our discussion of this passage with two observations. First, it is not convincing, and second, it is not clear what difference it could possibly make if it were true, and consequently, it is not entirely clear what it would mean for it to be true.

There are a number of different claims to be distinguished in this passage, some more plausible than others, even allowing for its premises (a finite number of forces and infinite time). As it stands, we are not persuaded either that a finite number of elements could not generate an infinite number of qualitatively different states, thus making the necessary infinite repetition of each state a non sequitor. Nor, if everything were to be repeated infinitely, can we see why it must take the form of exact cycles of complete sequences of permutations. While we are not the first to have had doubts about this proof, others have found it more acceptable. Danto, for example,[10] believes that with the addition of various other plausible premises it can be made to work. We shall argue, however, that Nietzsche does not need the precise repetitions that this argument, if successful, would prove. But first we shall look at another problem with the idea of eternal recurrence as so conceived: What would it mean for it to be true?

We can pose our worry like this: what would it be to be in one cycle rather than another? The request for some distinguishing feature by which one cycle could be distinguished from another must always be refused, for ex hypothesi there can be none without violating the principle that what returns does so identically. There is no point outside such a series to mark one's place. The hypothesis could not, then, be confirmed or refuted by our ordinary experience. Yet unlike the hypothesis of a divine being, it does not posit a transcendence, a higher plane of existence, just a horizontal extension of this one. Eternal recurrence is minimally, it seems, an untestable hypothesis, consistent with ordinary experience, requiring no higher being, and one the mere truth or falsity of which has no effect on our experience of the real world. It sounds like an empty, uninteresting idea which might at best occupy a marginal place in the dreams of an idle mind. And yet Nietzsche himself claims it to be his most powerful insight! Thus:

1 He claims (*The Will to power*, no.55) it is 'the most scientific hypothesis'. We shall have something to say about this shortly.

2 In the plan of the book on eternal recurrence (outlined in *The Will to Power*, no.1057), section 2 is entitled 'Proof of the doctrine'. He clearly takes the cosmological argument seriously.

3 He clearly contends that belief in eternal recurrence does make an enormous difference. In a letter to Overbeck he wrote, 'If it is true – or rather if it is believed to be true – then everything changes and turns around and *all* previous values are devalued.'[11]

What we propose is a strategy of reading Nietzsche's cosmological presentation of this doctrine which will both explain the importance with which he credits it and resolve some of the difficulties we have with it. First, Nietzsche is not just offering this proof of eternal recurrence in an intellectual vacuum. He is opposing it both to the traditional conceptions of nineteenth-century mechanism, and to the teleological conceptions of traditional theology. Let us take mechanism first. Nietzsche has a number of reservations about the idea of the world as a network of causes and effects. He is sceptical about the very concepts of 'cause' and 'effect' (as varieties of fiction). And if (as Kelvin argued) mechanism leads to a final state (entropy), it must, in infinite past time, have already reached it. As it clearly has not, mechanism must be false.

Coming from Nietzsche, and especially where they concern eternal recurrence, which was after all the subject of a vision (see below), these arguments raise certain questions of evaluation. Nietzsche is not parodying scientific discourse;[12] yet neither is he committed to its concepts, its assumptions, its standards. Indeed, he elsewhere pours scorn on those conclusions that need proving. What he is doing, surely, is showing how eternal recurrence can be argued for even in terms that he did not himself endorse.

Some sort of confirmation of his willingness to adopt such a strategy can be found in the way he handles the other main view to which eternal recurrence is opposed – theological teleology. In no.1062, for example, we find the following argument:

> If the world had a goal, it must have been reached. If there were for it some unintended final state, this must also have been reached. If it were in any way capable of a pausing and becoming fixed, of 'being', then all becoming would long since have come to an end, along with all thinking, all 'spirit'. The fact of 'spirit' as a form of becoming proves that the world has no goal, no final state, and is incapable of being.

The language here is surely that of theology. The argument can be constructed by substituting the opposition between Being and Becoming for that between Being and non-Being in Aquinas' Third Way. Where Aquinas argues that a necessary being must be posited to explain how, in infinite past time, we have not been swallowed up by a coincidence of non-Being, Nietzsche argues that the absence of a goal must be posited to explain how, in infinite past time, the universe did not cease all becoming. Aquinas did not think that such proofs were necessary, only convenient for some. No more did Nietzsche. That Nietzsche's attitude to the frame of references in which such arguments are constructed is something short of total commitment can surely be seen in their next paragraph in which he continues:

> The old habit . . . of associating a goal with every event and a guiding, creative God with the world is so powerful that it requires an effort for a thinker not to fall into thinking of the very aimlessness of the world as intended.

However, there is clearly a sense in which the cosmological version of eternal recurrence moves within this frame of reference. In my view the cosmological argument for eternal recurrence can be seen as subversive of both teleology and mechanism in that it can be shown to be no less plausible in the very same terms. And that is the point of my saying that this proof is not offered in an intellectual vacuum. It may be quite as important that it challenge the existing contenders for our intellectual assent as that it finally convince us in its own right.

The second consideration we would offer towards a more receptive reading of the proof of eternal recurrence is that it can be seen as an attempt to give a rigorous scientific justification for believing something which in a more general form we might find far more plausible. And Nietzsche himself at the beginning of the very passage from which this proof comes offers us just such an account of his 'new world conception' which depends, not on any detailed argument, but on a model of a closed economy of forces. Does Nietzsche really need more than this? He writes:

> The world exists; it is not something that becomes, not something that passes away. Or rather: it becomes, it passes away, but it has never begun to become and never ceased from passing away – it maintains itself in both. It lives on itself: its excrements are its food.[13]

It might, however, seem that repetition is entirely missing from this picture, which would make it deficient in a vital respect. As we shall see later, the abandonment of exact cycles is a price some think Nietzsche has to pay to give eternal recurrence psychological force. But for this picture to be sufficient we would have to find in the fact that becoming 'never ceases' a sufficient embodiment of becoming. We shall come back to this question.

We have cited Nietzsche's remark in a letter that, if it is believed true, eternal recurrence turns everything round. It might be suggested that a comparison with heavenly salvation would be appropriate here. For that too, true or not, makes an enormous difference if one believes it possible. And it shares the feature of unverifiability.

Heavenly salvation is usually thought of as a reward, or at least as a consequence of having led a certain sort of life. The reward is to be led to another life distinct from the first, one in which, one presumes, suffering is absent (or in the case of hell, in which suffering is eternal and hope is absent). In this case too, it is arguable that the truth or falsity of the existence of an afterlife has no direct bearing on the facts of this life, while belief in such a state can have an enormous 'effect'. Is eternal recurrence merely a kind of inversion of salvation? A kind of upsidedown theology?

Surely, on this first cosmological version, no. Because on this account it can be shown that the connection between one cycle and the next is neither causal nor moral, nothing I do will have the slightest effect on the next round. This is true whether I believe eternal recurrence or not. And furthermore, if one did suppose the relationship between one cycle and the next to be one of cause/effect in whatever loose form, one could not call it salvation (or damnation) for what one does merely to be *repeated* infinitely. Eternal recurrence does not offer a version of heaven or hell. It can offer in itself neither punishment nor reward. It is a horizontal move, not a vertical one. It is this feature – the horizontality of eternal recurrence – that, as we shall now explain, allows the cosmological version of eternal recurrence to play its special role in what we have called the transvaluation of our ordinary concept of time.

We seem to be able to think of eternal recurrence as a loopy arrow, as a single temporal series of a strange loopy shape.[14] Without departing from seriality, Nietzsche has thereby generated a structure which threatens it. When we talk of a loopy shape, we think representationally of something like a coil, a spring shape. On such a model we would possess a way of distinguishing between the different cycles, even if there were no clear point at which one cycle begins and ends. But on the cosmological model, there is no external point of vision, and indeed we are not simply dealing with a model. There is no way of distinguishing between one cycle and the next etc. We are, or are inside, the coil. We are, unlike Zarathustra's dwarf, *in* the gateway *Augenblick*, and to us the entire history of the universe as we know it *could* only seem a straight line, the arc of an immense circle.

Why do we labour this literal interpretation of the eternal recurrence as a cosmological hypothesis? Should we not simply feel its unfathomable power and not pause to analyse its reflective implications? We claim that this cosmological version is the first stage (or can be so construed) of Nietzsche's deconstruction of ordinary serial time. The key to this operation is that Nietzsche has managed to *construct*, using ordinary serial time, a plausible account of the structure of time which provides the basis for the transvaluation of that 'ordinary time'. Eternal recurrence seems merely to be a very powerful *modification or extension of seriality*. But in fact it puts in question the assumed self-contained status of its units – nows – and their fundamental successivity. For as well as being located on a horizontal axis of succession, each 'unit' also appears to be a member of a transversal series of repetitions.

Psychological time

It is hard to contain this version, as it appears in so many guises. Perhaps the *key* to it is the role of eternal recurrence in undermining and displacing the idea of *purpose* – be it personal or historical. As such, however, it is merely negative, and much more needs to be said about the idea of affirmation and the transformation of the will. We begin with an account of what we might call the 'intensity of the moment', which provides something of a template for self-affirmation.

The intensity of the moment

The cosmological version of eternal recurrence functions in such a way as to extend serial succession (in 'loops') so that each individual moment acquires membership of an additional, trans-versal series.[15] Consequently – and we take this up more fully in the next section – the identity of such units will also be divided along these two axes.

'Has time flow away? Have I not fallen . . . into the well of eternity?'[16] This second, quasi-vertical dimension to each moment, opens up the possibility of depth and, experientially, intensity. Let us first look at some of the formulations Nietzsche has given of 'the intensity of the moment'. Writing of the aesthetic moment of 'rapture', Nietzsche says, ' . . . in this condition one enriches everything out of one's own abundance: what one sees, what one desires, one sees swollen, pressing, strong, overladen with energy . . . '. He goes on: ' . . . the entire emotional system is alerted and intensified so that it discharges all its powers of representation, imitation, transfiguration, transmutation, every kind of mimicry and playacting conjointly . . . '[17] And the first published account Nietzsche gives of eternal recurrence[18] is the occasion for another depiction of a privileged moment. He imagines a demon suggesting that the 'eternal hourglass of existence is turned upside down again and again' and suggests two possible reactions – (a) utter despondency and misery, (b) exhilaration. The latter he puts like this: ' . . . or have you once experienced a tremendous moment when you would have answered him: "You are a god . . . "?'. Elsewhere[19] he tells of 'attaining' the *Übermensch* 'for one moment' and of the immortal 'moment . . . in which I produced return'.

The question I would like to put is this: how far are we confronted here with a new *general* account of the moment – and how far only of certain privileged moments? And, if the latter, in what way is Nietzsche offering a more general transvaluation of time? One thing must be true – any 'general account of time' must allow the possibility of these self-expansive moments. But are they special cases or the general rule? Clearly, at one level they must be special cases, or they could not exist distinctively, or in contrast to the depressive moments of anguish at the possibility of eternal recurrence. And yet I think it is clear that for Nietzsche they are special in a special sense – they realize the highest possibility of temporal experience – an intensity[20] of vision and/or self-mobilization and affirmation. But what of all the *other* moments that never achieve this status? Do we not have to accept that they too are part of time, so that we cannot say that Nietzsche's account of time *in general* is ecstatic and affirmative? Should we *just* say that he offers an ideal way of living (the moment), based on possibilities intermittently realized?

This would not be a dull view. Even taken by itself, it would require and justify some sort of existential temporality to accommodate these peak experiences. But we cannot rest with this picture, for a number of reasons:

1 The cosmological version of eternal recurrence has already compromised the idea of time *simply* as a sequence of distinct moments. The addition of a depth to each moment redirects our attention away from relations of succession towards the possibilities of intensification. When Nietzsche writes of the 'eternity' of the moment, this is not simply a reference to its infinite recurrence at other times. The picture we might have of life as a sequence of moments, some high, some low, still depends on giving seriality the last word. *Given that model*, leaping from peak to peak would correspond more closely to Nietzsche's picture. Yet Nietzsche does not retain that picture. The variable intensity of the eternally recurring moment constitutes an alternative. We return to this shortly.

2 There is a second crucial reason why these peak moments are not just different, but privileged in relation to those of the plains or the valleys. Part of what makes for the experience of exhilaration is that they project their own ecstatic affirmative vision onto the rest of time. If we think of time from within the ecstasy of such moment, then those moments that do not actualise this peak possibility simply do not figure. This gives us a way of understanding the eternity of the moment ('. . . joy wants the eternity of all things, wants deep, deep eternity') in a way quite different from, say, Goethe,[21] and in a way that seems to *conflict* with the supposition that in eternal recurrence *everything* returns, even the meanest. Here we approach Klossowski[22] and Deleuze's reading of the eternal return as a *selective* operation.

3 It is *possible* to argue that it is *not* the privilege of peak experiences that they project their own temporality onto the rest of time. Do not such experiences as boredom, depression, and self-destructive feelings do the same? But if they do so, there is a major difference. Only this affirmative rapture *wills itself enough* to will its own *infinite repetition*. Only this total self-affirmation wants itself more and again.

Let us now turn to the role of eternal recurrence in undermining and displacing the idea of purpose in psychological time – the transformation of the will.

The transformation of the will

If we consider that structure of action (and the temporality that underlies it) in which goals are pursued and ideals aimed at, it is hard to see it as avoidable, let alone as being flawed in some way. For Nietzsche, this simple structure – the pursuit of values – very easily takes a pathological form, which he calls nihilism. For the positing of ideals – especially those that could never quite be realized – is a tacit *devaluation* of this world. Plato, in this sense, is the consummate nihilist. Similarly, the belief in the perfectibility of man, utopian thinking, the search for truth, can be seen as valuations of the future, that, negatively, devalue the present. But the mere recognition of the negative nature of ordinary human values merely leads to a second stage of depressive nihilism, in which the world has no value, and there are no values for it to have. As we shall see, the thought of the eternal recurrence is meant to be able to take this crushing idea to its limit, and in so doing posing a challenge to our attitude to the past. For the will finds in the past an obstacle that it finds impossible to overcome: the past, it seems, is over, is not subject to my will, cannot be changed.

However in the section 'On Redemption' in *Thus Spoke Zarathustra* Nietzsche charts the course of the liberation of the will. In his *What is Called Thinking?* Heidegger devotes some five pages to a discussion of this section, in which, broadly speaking, he tries to show that the will's liberation consists in a triumphant victory over all obstacles by which victory it instates itself unchallenged in the seat of metaphysical subjectivity.[23] Zarathustra speaks to his disciples: '"Will – that is what the liberator and bringer of joy is called": thus I have taught you my friends. But now learn this as well: the will itself is still a prisoner.' Why is it still a prisoner? 'Powerless against that which has been done, the will is an angry spectator of all things past . . . it cannot break time and time's desire.'[24] There follows an account of a sequence of moves the will makes in revenge, as Nietzsche puts it, against this obstacle to its power, concluding with the position we could attribute to Schopenhauer and to Buddhism – that 'willing become not-willing'. Zarathustra's comment on this is as follows:

I led you away from these fable-songs when I taught you: 'The will is a creator.'

44

All 'It was' is a fragment, a riddle, a dreadful chance – until the creative will says to it: 'But I willed it thus.'
The will that is the will to power must will something higher than any reconciliation – but how shall that happen? Who has taught it to will backwards too?[25]

The question is left unanswered. Zarathustra 'looked like a man seized by extreme terror'. It will turn out, of course, that the *Übermensch* is the answer to the question.

My view is that this sentence: 'The will that is the will to power must will something higher than any reconciliation' – which Heidegger does not to my knowledge allude to – poses a difficulty for his reading of Nietzsche's account as a metaphysics of will. What Nietzsche is insisting on is that the aim of this new *creative* willing is not merely reconciliation to the necessity of time's passing away, but an active affirmation of the fact. The question is whether this affirmative willing can genuinely exceed the identity-seeking, reconciling, appropriating gestures characteristic of the rationalizations which had preceded it.[26]

Clearly, this transformation of the will already subverts what I have called 'ordinary motivational time'. We are to will, not just accept, but *will* what has been, and the fact that time will continue to pass over into the past. This is an idea it is almost impossible to to think. One can accept that it might in theory satisfy the condition of going beyond mere reconciliation, but what can it mean? The idea *sticks* there, undecidable in terms of our ordinary understanding of willing, and will not go away.

I mentioned before the importance for Nietzsche of a transformation of nihilism – he saw himself as moving beyond nihilism only in the late work, *Ecce Homo* – and in this move, we find the greatest challenge to our ordinary understanding of motivation. The thought of eternal recurrence has two faces: a face of terror and a face of exhilaration. The *test* that eternal recurrence poses is whether one can say yes to it, and transcend terror as well as *ressentiment*. 'Courage', Nietzsche writes 'destroys even death, for it says "Was *that* life? Well then, once more."'[27] But the passage I have just been alluding to is Nietzsche's first real announcement of the eternal recurrence.

When one first grasps eternal recurrence, all hope is extinguished. Everything incomplete, ill-formed, unwanted, will return. But there follows an *expansion*, 'a tremendous moment', in which one finds oneself strong enough to affirm *all* this. We learn something, I believe, from Nietzsche's precise words: '*If this thought gained possession of you, it would change you* as you are, or perhaps crush you', or 'What does not kill me makes me stronger' – as he wrote in *Twilight of the Idols*.[28]

The idea of eternal recurrence is both a test of one's strength, and also a source, an inspiration. The demon, on the second reading, is recognized as 'a god'. The idea can 'take possession'. At this most vital point, Nietzsche is taking as seriously as he could the idea that the consequences of believing something are more important than its truth (if indeed they can be distinguished from it). Eternal recurrence may be a trial; it is also a ladder.

But can it really *make sense* to believe it? In this form? And could it, after all, really make any difference, except by a misunderstanding? We have already come across these questions – they are important in their own right, but also for judging whether Nietzsche has really succeeded in displacing the ordinary motivational time we usually take for granted.

There are at least two ways of articulating a critical attitude to the value or significance of eternal recurrence, arguing 1. That eternal recurrence cannot make any difference because (as we saw above) we will never have any memory of past cycles, nor will our actions ever *affect* future cycles. Indeed it could be said that experientially it makes no difference whether I do this self-same thing once or an infinite number of times, if each time is independent of the other, and each occasion is identical; or 2. That it makes an enormous difference, because if the doctrine is true then I have no real possibility of transforming, or transvaluing anything, unless, of course, I have already done so before. This view Nietzsche calls 'Turkish fatalism'.

When one reads commentaries on Nietzsche, and indeed Nietzsche himself, one is given the impression that these questions have sadly 'missed the point'. Two different general responses are offered, which are not, in my view, mutually consistent. The first, Nietzsche's own, which applies both to fatalism and also to the indifferentism of the first objection, is basically a form of compatibilism.

The truth is that every man himself is a piece of fate; when he thinks he is stirring against fate in the way described, fate is being realized here, too; the struggle is imaginary, but so is resignation to fate – all these imaginary ideas are *included* in fate.

You yourself, poor frightened man, are the invincible Moira reigning far above the gods . . . In you the whole future of the human world is predetermined – it will not help you if you are terrified of yourself.[29]

But the second explanation of why they are misplaced involves a further step away from the idea of eternal recurrence as a scientific hypothesis about repetitive cycles. The eternal recurrence is neither a mechanical nor 'logical' nor mathematical 'repetition'. Rather it can exercise a *selective* power. This selectivity can be understood in two different ways: one 'moral' and the other ontological. The first, 'moral', way is the more obvious. On this account, only what can affirm its infinite repetition *deserves* to return. Clearly, such an idea can function as a principle by which one regulates one's words and deeds, a kind of superviligant conscience. The ability to affirm eternal recurrence is a moral test. Nietzsche clearly offers us this version, but it has its difficulties. It seems to leave open the prospect of a *gap* between what ought to happen and what does. This is especially true if we take seriously the idea that actually *everything*, deserving or not, returns. And the problem is that for Nietzsche, such a gap *invites nihilism*.[30] The second, less obvious way, we will call 'ontological'. On this account, willing eternal recurrence *actually does* operate as a selective procedure, such that certain events, objects, relations, moments will return and some will not. Clearly this is a significant modification of the original cosmological account of eternal recurrence. And just as obviously there are difficulties with it. For a start, it undercuts the heroism of the original affirmation that wills the return even of the lowliest and meanest thing. For such things would no longer return at all.

There are two rather different ways of thinking through this second alternative. The first would concentrate on such Nietzschean remarks as that the thought of eternal recurrence licenses most men to self-erasure (crushed by 'the greatest weight'). There will be some people who continue who affirm themselves and the world, and some also – at least for a time – who do not. (I take it this can be understood either physically or existentially.)[31] But here 'continue' is relative to a particular life, and, on the *standard* version of eternal recurrence, those acts (or conditions) of self-erasure would themselves return eternally just as much as the acts of self-overcoming. And that would surely spoil the story. The second way of pursuing the *ontological* version of selectivity is not wholly distinct, but conceptually far more subtle.

Deleuze[32] argues that if (a) we take seriously the idea that eternal recurrence is 'the being of becoming' (as Nietzsche himself claims),[33] and (b) we distinguish (as Nietzsche does) between 'active' and 'reactive' (forces) and apply this distinction to kinds of 'becoming'; then (c) we can say that only 'active becoming' 'has being' in the sense of embodying the principle of eternal recurrence. So, (d) only *active* becoming returns. Why? Deleuze: 'the eternal return would become contradictory if it were the return of *re*active forces'.[34]

The work here is obviously being done by the relation between being and becoming, and we must defer until the next section a proper assessment of this position. What we can say is that in Deleuze we find for the first time an account of how eternal recurrence would function as a selective principle that does not obviously presuppose the ordinary model of time as a succession of point instants. The question we will now pose is this: what understanding can we have of the moment that will allow the return of only those moments which affirm themselves, or perhaps better, in which we affirm ourselves. The clue must lie in a way of thinking of time that leaves seriality – and thus revenge – behind.

'Ontological' time

I have suggested that the clue to how we can understand 'the moment' in such a way as to allow the return only of those moments in which we affirm ourselves lies in a way of thinking about time that leaves seriality behind. But how is such a thought to be realized? Would we not be trapped in a perpetual present? Consider the following: 1. What is at issue, what is valuable, what is at *stake* in any experience, is *always the same* – it is the intensity of self-affirmation that it contains. In this sense, other moments, moments that don't make the grade, simply do not come into the reckoning. 2. If we ask of 'the moment' whether it is one or many, we find ourselves embroiled in the most difficult thoughts. It is not enough to distinguish qualitative and numerical senses; we are left with, and I think Nietzsche means to leave us with, a genuine 'undecidable'. I would like to spend a little time on this, focussing on a famous passage from *Thus Spoke Zarathustra* ('Of the Vision and the Riddle') in which Nietzsche explains the eternal return in relation to the gateway called 'Moment', where the paths of the infinite past and the infinite future meet. The account proceeds in tones of increasing horror, and then turns to the vision of the shepherd choking on a snake, who bites off its head and is a transformed being. Let us look at this famous text:[35]

Then something occurred which lightened me: for the dwarf jumped from my shoulder, the inquisitive dwarf! And he squatted down upon a stone in front of me. But a gateway stood just where we had halted. 'Behold this gateway, dwarf!' I went on: 'It has two aspects. Two paths come together: no one has ever reached their end.'

'This long lane ahead of us – that is another eternity. They are in opposition to one another, these paths; they abut on one another: and it is here at this gateway that they come together. The name of the gateway is written above it: "Moment".'

'But if one were to follow them further and ever further and further: do you think, dwarf, that these paths would be in eternal opposition?'

'Everything straight lies', murmured the dwarf disdainfully.

'All truth is crooked, time itself is a circle.'

'Spirit of gravity!' I said angrily, 'do not treat this too lightly! . . .'

'Behold this moment!' I went on.

'From this gateway Moment a long eternal lane runs *back*: an eternity lies behind us.'

'Must not all things that *can* run have already run along this lane? Must not all things that *can* happen have already happened, been done, run past?'

'And if all things have been here before: what do you think of this moment, dwarf? Must not this gateway, too, have been here before?'

'And are not all things bound fast together in such a way that this moment draws after it all future things? *Therefore* draws itself too?'[36]

Three sections of this passage deserve special comment: 1. 'They are in opposition to each other, these paths . . . and it is here at this gateway that they come together.' 2. ' . . . what do you think of this moment, dwarf? Must not this gateway, too, have been here before? And are not all things bound fast together in such a way that this moment draws after it all future things? *Therefore* draws itself too?' 3. 'The name of the gateway is written above it: "Moment".'

We first note that the moment is the *coming together* of two paths (past and future) in opposition. And yet this *coming together* is not as such a reconciliation, but a tension. Future and past *abut*, they *affront* one another. It is left to the possibility of eternal recurrence to alleviate their oppositional character. Second, the question of the gateway. When Zarathustra asks 'Must not this gateway, too, have been here before?' is he talking of *this particular* moment, or is he talking of the moment as the basis of a structure of repetition? What would it be to talk of *this* moment, to *talk* of this moment? Nietzsche has already given it metaphorical substantiality by calling it a *gateway*. And we can suppose that the vertical parts of the gateway will symbolize the quasi-vertical dimension of time. But there is a third point.

It is a commonplace of the structuralist view of language to suppose that it has to be understood as comprising two axes – syntagmatic/paradigmatic, metonymic/metaphoric etc.[37] The serial articulations of a word are supplemented by paradigmatic relationships of substitutability – relationships in which substitutions of other words would retain some important feature, some meaning, some grammatical category, still forming an intelligible sentence, etc. Now it might be thought gratuitous to suggest a parallel between the double axis of language, and the double axis of time that eternal recurrence would generate. But consider the sentence 'The name of the gateway is *written* above it: "Moment".' At this critical point, Nietzsche introduces not just 'language' but writing. What is the force of this appearance of writing? It is tempting to compare it to that point in the first chapter in Hegel's *Phenomenology of Spirit* at which he is demonstrating that 'the universal is the truth of sense-certainty'. He writes:

> It is as a universal . . . that we *give utterance* to sensuous fact. What we say is 'this', i.e. the universal *this*. We do not *present before* our mind in saying so the universal this, or being in general, but we *utter* what is universal; language, as we see, is the more truthful.[38]

For Hegel, the moment of language is the moment of universality. Can we say the same of Nietzsche – for example, in 'Truth and Lie in an Extra-Moral Sense'? Is not Nietzsche suggesting that the structure of 'moment' is as independent of any particular experience as is writing of any particular intentional context? Might it not then be that it is precisely the *moment* that eternally returns the same? But what is the moment? When he writes '*this* gateway' should we read it as one or as many? It is tempting to read him as saying there is just one moment, but then we have to add 'which gets repeated'. So there are many.

I would suggest first of all that the moment of writing in Nietzsche, as in Hegel's reference to the 'utterance' of 'this', puts in question the *presence* of consciousness ('We do not present before our mind in saying so the universal this.') But with Nietzsche, we are not, as with Hegel, led to another presence – that of the realm of universality (which will ultimately be subsumed under that general self-presence of spirit). For Nietzsche, the moment of writing is the moment of undecidability; undecidability, that is, as always, within the framework that insists on a clear answer to the question of metaphysics – one or many?

We can recall here Nietzsche's suggestion that eternal recurrence is 'the being of becoming', or 'the closest approximation of being in becoming'. Abstractly, it might suggest (and we might conclude) that eternal recurrence is the way the force of becoming is finally *betrayed*. Becoming, we might say, is the one thing that never changes, and hence embodies the value of *permanence*, which is the hallmark of Being.

Is there not something very strange about such a formulation? 'Becoming is the one thing that never changes' seems like a perfectly intelligible sentence. But what if becoming were the greatest threat to all thinking involving an 'is'? The 'approximation' of the becoming of eternal recurrence to being should be read neither as Nietzsche's confession of a new metaphysics, nor as a naïve admission of that fact.

Rather, the approximation of the becoming of eternal recurrence to being should be seen as a disruptive *substitution of an undecidable term* into metaphysical discourse. 'Becoming' in Nietzsche functions in the way in which, for example, 'writing' functions in Derrida.[39] Becoming is no more in simple opposition to Being than *writing* (in Derrida's new sense) can be simply *opposed* to speech.[40] The function of eternal recurrence is to allow the reinscription of becoming within the discourse of metaphysics in a way that *undermines* that discourse.

The point is that becoming demands a quite 'different' logic of identity from that of being.

It is now possible, I think, to distinguish more clearly three quite different functions of eternal recurrence. The first, as I have suggested, undermines the privilege of seriality by introducing, via exact cycles, a quasi-vertical depth. The second is to parody the values of a philosophy of being, by providing for every particular a kind of universality. But there is a third function, and that will require yet another thinking through of the meaning of eternal recurrence.[41]

We have already heard what Nietzsche has to say about the state of rapture as an affirmative projectivity. The Dionysian poet could be said to 'go out of himself',[42] and when Nietzsche discusses the will to power, he says 'it must will something *higher than any reconciliation*'. In each case the basic structure is one of a *self-exceeding* which is not appropriated, but which, precisely, *risks* the self, and does *not* aim at a higher reconciliation. This, I would argue, is the fundamental structure of the *moment* for Nietzsche. And corresponding to this futural element of *risk* is the importance of *forgetting*; both are aspects of non-appropriative thought.

How is this idea of a self-exceeding that is not appropriated compatible with talk of the eternal recurrence of the same?[43] Does not the reference to sameness imply, if not identity, at least a continuity? And is that not precisely what is put in question by an exceeding that does not 'return'?

One 'philological' matter makes such compatibility more plausible than it might at first seem: in the very notebook where the idea of eternal recurrence is first sketched out,[44] Nietzsche distributes among his notes on *ewige Wiederkehr des Gleichen* a whole series of notes that criticize – in a devastating way – the very postulation of any *das Gleiche* in either science or philosophy. What then can the 'same' possibly mean in eternal recurrence?

There is a way of reading this reference to the eternal return of the 'same' that does make sense. We can treat it as a description not of repeated *contents* of experience but of the dynamic structure of experience – the rhythm, the pulse of excitement and fatigue, of arousal and consummation, of exhilaration and passivity, of the rising and setting of the passions. It is this *movement*, the movement of becoming, that is repeated eternally. Or, with Deleuze,[45] we can say that it is *the returning that returns*.

But what of our reference to a non-appropriating exceeding, a non-reconciliatory will? Surely the point is that sameness is not what is repeated, not what returns, but, again, what is constituted by that return. The 'return to self' operates without a self, *is* the self.[46] Sameness is this eternal recurrence. Eternal recurrence is the condition of and not merely the extension or prolongation of sameness.

I now want to return to the question with which I began – whether Nietzsche's thought is another kind of philosophy of presence or whether he might be said to have *exceeded* the parameters of that framework. Without wanting to claim to have mastered the complexities of Heidegger's reading of Nietzsche, it is worth reminding ourselves that Heidegger does claim that Nietzsche's philosophy is in this way metaphysical. The will that wills the past, that affirms all that has been and which is then able to will 'the eternal return of the same' is, he says, 'the supreme triumph of the metaphysics of the will that eternally wills its own willing'.[47] This will to power is interpreted as a form – the highest form – of subjectivity, of self-presence. But surely everything could turn on how we think of the moment? And surely the *very least* we can say about Heidegger's interpretation is that when he interprets the closure of the ring of recurrence as *downgoing* he puts in question his own insistence that Nietzsche's is a metaphysics of the will.

If Nietzsche's account of the moment renders its relation to the question 'one or many' undecidable, and if the ecstatic moment can be treated not as an *exception* but simply as the highest possible intensification of experience, and if the realization of that possibility is, as I believe it is for Nietzsche, the essence (i.e. non-essence) of time, there surely is a case for saying that Nietzsche's thought here at least aims beyond presence and self-presence. Everything hangs on our being able to accept the idea that (a) a general description can be given of the various accounts Nietzsche gives of the intensities of a moment; and (b) that this description is that of a willing/thinking/affirming beyond, that does *not* aim at its own preservation, but risks itself perpetually, a going out that, even as it anticipates a *return*, puts in question what it is that will be returned to.

Such a reading would take the interpretation of Nietzsche to a certain limit, and is undoubtedly itself 'selective'. For, as Derrida might say, deconstructive theses coexist in Nietzsche with those that remain inscribed within metaphysics.

Reading Heidegger reading Nietzsche: an interim report

Clearly a challenge is being posed here to Heidegger's reading of Nietzsche, and we devote this last section to an all too perfunctory elaboration of that challenge. We continue to draw on the work of Deleuze to that end. Unlike Heidegger, he sees the concepts of Will to Power and Eternal Recurrence as successfully deconstructing the matrix of metaphysical conceptuality. And it may be with Heidegger in mind that he writes 'We misinterpret the expression "eternal return" if we understand it as 'return of the same".' To readers of Derrida, his argument will be familiar, although the direction it gives to the thought of the eternal recurrence is new. He writes: 'The synthetic relation of the moment to itself as present, past and future grounds its relation to other moments. The eternal return is thus an answer to the problem of passage.' (ibid.) We shall return to discuss this passage (together with 'The Vision and the Riddle') shortly. Deleuze continues: 'And in this sense it must not be interpreted as the return of something that is, that is "one", or the "same". We misinterpret the expression "eternal return" if we understand it as "return of the same".' (ibid.) We must prepare ourselves for an inversion:

It is not being that returns but rather the returning itself that constitutes being insofar as it is affirmed of becoming, and of that which passes. It is not some one thing which returns but rather returning itself is the one thing which is affirmed of diversity or multiplicity. In other words, *identity in eternal return does not describe the nature of that which returns but*, on the contrary, *the fact of returning for that which differs.* This is why the eternal return must be thought of as a synthesis, a synthesis of time and its dimensions, a synthesis of diversity, and its reproduction . . . (ibid.) (our emphasis).

Derrida's position seems very similar here. He writes: 'And on the basis of this unfolding of the same as *differance* we see announced the sameness of *differance* and repetition in the eternal return.'[49] For both Deleuze and Derrida the key underlying idea is that identity is not a fixed point we need to presuppose for differences to be possible; matters are rather the other way round. And the possibility that a thing can appear again and again at different times is what *gives it* an identity; it is not dependent on it having a prior atemporal identity. Time, then, is not only *constitutive* of identity, rather than a mere medium in which things unfold, but is *itself* constituted by its role in supporting identities and differences. But even if we cannot in any simple way say 'what' it is that returns, independently of its returning, there *are* still questions that need answering. Perhaps I can put my disquiet like this: when Deleuze talks of 'the returning itself that constitutes being' is he talking here in fact of Being or beings? Is he referring to Time itself, or to things in time? I take it that Nietzsche fairly plainly talks about things in time, or if not things at least events, configurations of forces. And yet if we take seriously these remarks of Deleuze, eternal return is being interpreted as the ground of 'time itself'. It may or may not be possible to square this with any account of the return of particular (especially non-human) beings, but it would certainly suggest that, yet again, eternal recurrence is functioning as a device for the deconstruction of time – here time seen as the locus of identity.

Here Deleuze raises explicitly the question with which we began – that of presence. I suggested at the outset that Nietzsche might perhaps have offered an account of the present, and indeed of time based on the present, that was not subject to Heidegger's (or to Derrida's) criticisms. The vital question will undoubtedly be the status of *becoming* in Nietzsche. Let us now begin to open up this question.

Heidegger's verdict on Nietzsche is rather different from that of either Deleuze or Derrida. Heidegger quotes Nietzsche's remark 'that *everything recurs* is the closest approximation of a world of Becoming to one of Being – peak of meditation'[50] and comments, 'with his doctrine of eternal return, Nietzsche in his way thinks nothing else than the thought that pervades the whole of western philosophy'.[51]
Why? Because he thinks Being as Time without thinking it as the *question* of Being.

Eternity, not as a static 'now', nor as a sequence of 'nows' rolling off into the infinite, but as the 'now' that bends back into itself: what is that if not the concealed essence of Time? Thinking Being, Will to Power, as eternal return, thinking the most difficult thought of philosophy means thinking Being as Time.[52]

So, Nietzsche does not think of the *question* of Being (and Time). But might one not justly respond that the *thought* of eternal return is a continuous questioning, that to use such an idea as an explication of time as Becoming, is to lodge a question as deep as possible into the heart of time. It may be that when understood as 'the mere bending back of the "now"' the eternal return no longer had that disturbing undecidability that we have consistently noted, but perhaps that is a deficiency in Heidegger's reading. Might not Deleuze be right to query any and every reading of eternal return as (always) eternal return of the same? Furthermore, if our presentation of Nietzsche's break with Aristotelian and Augustinian accounts of time is correct, then surely Nietzsche could be said to have anticipated Heidegger's own de-structuring of the history of Being (and Time) as well as Heidegger's own ecstatic account of temporality.

Of course, Heidegger denies Nietzsche these achievements. In *What is Called Thinking?*[53] he claims that ' . . . the answer Aristotle gave to the question of the essential nature of time still governs Nietzsche's idea of time'. We have already alluded to his argument: that Nietzsche's use of a transvaluing will to affirm that past betrays a traditional valuation of Being (including the 'Being' of time) as present. Our response, we may recall, was to say that he took no account of Nietzsche's reference to a will that did not seek 'reconciliation' – that Heidegger was *refusing* the radicality of Nietzsche's affirmative willing.

Finally, I would like to suggest a way of reading Heidegger on Nietzsche that develops some of the ambiguities in the notion of authenticity to be found in Heidegger's *Being and Time*. Heidegger's discussion of authenticity moves between tendencies towards closure (for example, the idea that one's 'ownmost possibilities' could ever be anything more than a question), and tendencies that would preclude such a closure, such as references to anxiety, the abyss, and throwness.[54] I would like to suggest that this tension between these two motifs is not just found generally in *Being and Time*, but is found *specifically* connected with the question of that ongoing rupturing of selfhood that I have associated with the Nietzschean moment. Even more interestingly,

Heidegger offers us, within the space of a few lines, though without posing it *as* a problem, the very question that is most pressing – how to understand this 'rupturing' in terms of Being. Finally, he does this at one of the very few places at which he invokes the name (in brackets!) of Nietzsche. These are the sentences in question:

1. Anticipation discloses to existence that its uttermost possibility lies in *giving itself up*, and thus it shatters all one's tenaciousness to whatever existence one has reached.[55]

What is this 'giving itself up' (*Selbstaufgabe*)? Is it just death in the narrow sense, or is it not precisely the risking of all one is and has known? How does Heidegger continue? Doesn't he temper the radicality of the suggestion he has just made?

2. In anticipation, *Dasein* guards itself against falling back behind itself and behind the potentiality for Being which it is understood. It guards itself against 'becoming too old for its victories' (Nietzsche). (ibid.)

The important thing here is how we understand 'falling back behind oneself' and the 'potentiality for Being' (which it has understood).

These remarks can be given a direct Nietzschean interpretation – the 'understanding of Being' which *Dasein* has understood is not a self to which one clings, but, I would suggest, a grasp of the sense and responsibility of the 'intensity' of experience. The problem about 'not falling back' is the same problem as that of 'selectivity'. Only what can will its own return can/should return.

The clear Nietzschean influences here suggests what will seem obvious when stated – that we would be wise not to divorce Heidegger's reading of Nietzsche from his continuing attempts at a self-interpretation.[56]

I would like to have shown that if we suppose that the model of Dionysian excess provides a standard by which to measure the intensity of the moment, and if that excess is a non-recuperable rupture with all 'presence', then Nietzsche's 'moment', so far from being the reworking of the metaphysical value of presence, is the scene of its explosion.

Is that what we should conclude about Nietzsche? Does he achieve the magical result of a non-metaphysical philosophy of the present?

Perhaps matters are not quite so clear cut. What he does do, I believe, is force us to make a distinction between two levels at which we can understand the meaning of 'presence' as a metaphysical value. The first we might in modern terms call foundationalist, and the second we could call appropriative. To each corresponds a different stratum of that mode of textual inscription which makes for metaphysics. By foundationalist I mean a kind of thinking that reduces to or derives from one fundamental point the entire developed structure of some theoretical field. Arguably, Nietzsche does this at least in a formal, and perhaps only strategic way, if we are right in giving the moment the status we have. Nonetheless we could say, in Levinasian language, that for Nietzsche, time, in the shape of this 'moment' is an opening onto the other, onto otherness, onto what may never be appropriated, made identical, brought back. Here Nietzsche does break with the second characterisation we have given of the metaphysical value associated with presence.

This characterisation brings back the question we raised when discussing whether Nietzsche's was a special or a general theory. And for all the value of seeing the ecstatic moment as an idea, it surely does not *actually* capture the general structure of time. It is precisely because it does not that it can function as an ideal. And what that suggests is that we may learn more about the possibilities of exceeding metaphysics from the non-appropriative stratum of his thinking than from its putative foundationalism.

Notes

1 See ch.3 of J. Derrida, *Of Grammatology*, trans. G.C. Spivak, Baltimore, Johns Hopkins, 1980

2 Nietzsche uses two different expressions – 'return' (*Wiederkunft*) and 'recurrence' (*Wiederkehr*). One could use these expressions to mark a strict distinction – between the recurrence of events and the return of people or things. But no such systematic usage is found in Nietzsche, and my various use of these two terms reflects the preferred terms of different commentators on Nietzsche at different times. Joan Stambaugh, whose book, *Nietzsche's Thought of Eternal Return* is one of the best things written on the subject, further points out (pp.29–31) that in his critical passages, Nietzsche usually uses the expression *Widerkunft* and that he hardly ever talks of *Wiederholung*

(repetition), which, again, suggests that exact reruns were not part of his favoured version of eternal return.

3 See D.C. Wood, *The Deconstruction of Time*, Humanities/MacMillan, Atlantic Highlands/London, forthcoming (1988). This essay is substantially drawn from the first chapter of that book.

4 See, for example, 'The Intoxicated Song' (*Das trunkene Lied*), the penultimate section of the fourth and last part of *ASZ*. References will be to the Penguin edition translated by R.J. Hollingdale, 1961.

5 A selection of Nietzsche's unpublished writings – his *Nachlass* – was assembled under the title of *Der Wille zur Macht* (1901). I quote in this paper from the Hollingdale and Kaufmann translation of *The Will to Power*, New York, Vintage (Random House), 1968. The section containing the most important attempt at a scientific proof is 1066, see below.

6 An excellent paper by Robin Small, 'Three Interpretations of Eternal Recurrence', *Dialogue* XXII, 1983, pp.91–112, makes this point more systematically.

7 The original title of this essay was to have been 'Nietzsche's Deconstruction of Time'. I have been persuaded that this may be too loose a use of the term to justify the prominence that a place in the title would give it. But there are parallels with even the technical account Derrida gives of the general strategy of deconstruction (in *Positions*, Paris, Editions de Minuit, 1972). I will suggest that Nietzsche reinscribes 'becoming' in a way parallel to the way Derrida reinscribes 'writing'. I claim, too, that the concept of eternal recurrence is undecidable in terms of the framework it puts in question.

8 In fact many crucial notes on eternal recurrence as 'cosmological' thought appear in notebook M III 1, dated Spring–Autumn 1881. For this and other references to Nietzsche's notebooks I am indebted to David Farrell Krell.

9 *WM*, no.1066

10 Arthur Danto, 'The Eternal Recurrence', in *Nietzsche: a Collection of Critical Essays*, ed. Robert Solomon, Garden City, Doubleday, 1973

11 The letter is dated 8 March 1884, cited by Stambaugh, op. cit. supra.

12 It is quite true that Nietzsche was strongly and positively influenced by Lange's *Geschichte des Materialismus* (1863), but I prefer to treat such positivistic and scientific streaks as there are in Nietzsche as weapons in an anti-metaphysical struggle rather than as beliefs strongly held in their own right. Causal determinism, for example, would be hard to square with his account of causation in 'The Four Great Errors' in *Twilight of the Idols*. Where Nietzsche's rhetorical and scientific tendencies clash, we favour the former.

13 *WM*, 1066

14 The association of time with loopy structures is of course not confined

to philosphical texts. See ch.XX ('Strange Loops, Or Tangled Hierarchies') of Douglas B. Hofstadter's extraordinary *Gödel, Escher, Bach*, Harvester, Brighton, 1979. And Faulkner (in *As I Lay Dying*) describes the rope cast by the Bundrens across the surging river to take their Mother's coffin across as follows: 'It is as though the space between us were time: an irrevocable quality. It is as though time, no longer running straight before us in a diminishing line, now runs parallel between us like a looping string, the distance being the doubling accretion of the thread and not the interval between.' Section 34, 'Darl'.

15 And the significance of the horizontal axis – the serial order of time – is itself compromised by the addition of the second. A parallel to Nietzsche's construction of an account that is deconstructive in its effects, by a simple modification of seriality, can be found in the Moebius strip, beloved of Lacan, in which the absolute difference between the two sides of a ribbon is transformed into a continuity merely by a twist and a join.

16 'At Noontide' in *ASZ* IV, translation p.288

17 See *GD*, 'Expeditions of an Untimely Man' no.9. See also Heidegger's *Nietzsche*, vol.1, section 14, 'Rapture as Aesthetic State'

18 *FW* no.341

19 The reference here (*Nachlass* XIV: 306; XII:371) are taken from Stambaugh (op. cit.) p.23

20 In this word 'intensity' we should hear the work of condensation (which latter word is itself a kind of intensification) – primarily of the ideas of *tension* and concentrated focus, a felt intensity – ideas that both inhabit and displace a psychological interpretation in so far as they suggest all sorts of difficulties with any traditionally substantive account of the 'subject'.

21 'The eternal is present with us in every moment; the transitoriness of time causes us no suffering', quoted by Karl Lowith in his *From Hegel to Nietzsche*, trans. David Green, Garden City, Doubleday, 1967, p.211

22 Pierre Klossowski, *Nietzsche et le Cercle Vicieux*, Paris, Mercure de France, 1969

23 For Nietzsche, Heidegger writes, and clearly with Schelling in mind,

Will is primal being. The highest product of primal being is eternity. The primal being of beings is the will, as the eternally recurrent willing of the eternal recurrence of the same. The eternal recurrence of the same is the supreme triumph of the metaphysics of the will that eternally wills its own willing. (*What is Called Thinking?*, Lecture X, p.104.)

I would also refer the reader to that most subtle discussion of Heidegger's appraisal of Nietzsche's 'metaphysics of the will' in ch.8

('The Last Thinker of the West', esp. pp.132–5) of David Farrell Krell's *Intimations of Mortality*, Penn State U.P., University Park/ London 1986

24 *ASZ* II, 'Of Redemption', translation p.161

25 Ibid.

26 This problem is plausibly represented by Vincent Descombes in his *Le Meme et l'Autre* Paris, Minuit, 1979 (translated as *Modern French Philosophy*, Cambridge, Cambridge Univerity Press, 1980) as *the* problem inherited by the 'désirants' – the French philosophers who took up Nietzsche's problems in the seventies – especially Deleuze, Lyotard and Klossowski.

27 *ASZ* III, 'Of the Vision and the Riddle', translation, p.178

28 'Maxims and Arrows', 8

29 I am grateful, again, to J. Stambaugh, *Nietzsche's Though of Eternal Return* for this quotation.

30 Vincent Descombes (see n.26 above) argues brilliantly that this problem haunts French Nietzscheans and that they do not escape its grip.

31 We could find here a parallel in Heidegger's account of authenticity and his contrast between finding oneself and forever losing oneself.

32 Giles Deleuze, *Nietzsche et la Philosophie*, Paris, Press Universitaires de France, 1962 (trans. Hugh Tomlinson, *Nietzsche and Philosophy*, London, Athlone, 1983)

33 *WM* no.617

34 *Nietzsche and Philosophy*, p.72

35 For Heidegger's reading of this passage see sections 6–8, 24 of Martin Heidegger, *Nietzsche*, vol.2, *The Eternal Return of the Same*, trans. David Farrell Krell, Harper and Row, New York, 1984

36 See n.23

37 The *locus classicus* of this view is probably Roman Jakobson's (with Morris Halle) *The Fundamentals of Language* (in particular 'Two Aspects of Language: Metaphor and Metonymy'), The Hague, Mouton, 1956.

38 G.F. Hegel, *Phenomenology of Spirit*, trans. A.V. Miller, Oxford, Clarendon, 1977, p.152

39 See the early essays in *Of Grammatology*, especially 'The End of the Book and the Beginning of Writing', and 'Linguistics and Grammatology'.

40 The non-dialectical possibilities of Nietzsche's thought rest on such a relation.

41 See n.17

42 See John Sallis' paper in this volume, and some aspects of David Pollard's.

43 See Deleuze, op. cit., (translation) p.48

44 See note 8

45 Op. cit

46 One could usefully compare Kierkegaard's position here, when he writes (*Sickness Unto Death*) that the Self is the relation that relates itself to itself.

47 *What is Called Thinking?* trans. John Macquarrie and Edward Robinson, Oxford, Blackwell, 1962, p.104

48 Deleuze, (trans), p.48

49 'Differance' (*Margins of Philosophy*, p.17)

50 M. Heidegger, *Nietzsche*, 2 vols. Pfullingen, Neske, 1961, translated in 4 vols. by David Farrell Krell, New York, Harper and Row, 1979–1982. These remarks come from vol.1 section 4, 'The Unity of Will to Power, Eternal Recurrence and Revaluation', p.19.

51 Ibid.

52 Ibid., p.20

53 *What is Called Thinking?*, p.101

54 I owe these thoughts (and much more) to discussions with John Llewelyn and David Farrell Krell

55 *Being and Time*, H264

56 There are very many of these: 'Way Back into the Fundamental Ground of Metaphysics', his 'Letter on Humanism', 'Time and Being', etc.

· 4 ·

Self-annihilation and Self-overcoming: Blake and Nietzsche

DAVID POLLARD

There are a number of similarities in the works of Blake and Nietzsche. Both wrote dithyrambic verse as well as rhyme. Both believed in the superabundance of creative energy. Both philosophised with a hammer. Both wrote prophetic books as a result of living in a destitute age. Both had backgrounds of religious conservatism and both thought that their attitude towards religion and creativity was an annihilation or an overcoming of Selfhood. It is with some justification that Blake has been called Nietzschean and Nietzsche a Romantic.

Blake

Throughout Blake's writings there exists a tension between Milton and Jesus, a tension which manifests itself already in his earliest work. This tension is, as it is in Nietzsche, anti-Christian. In the three plates of 1788, Blake argues against the Christian/Platonic teaching that appetite is evil and should be controlled by reason which is good: 'That Energy, called Evil, is alone from the Body & that Reason Call'd Good is alone from the soul.'[1] and: 'That God will torment Man in Eternity for following his Energies.'[2] But, even as early as this, Blake is rejecting these simple dichotomies: 'Man has no Body distinct from the soul.'[3]

Although 'Energy is the only life', 'Reason is the Bound or outward circumference of Energy.'[4] In the unitary man (*Einzelne*) Reason is the true form of Energy. We misconstrue when we destroy the relation between the terms. True Reason is the Contrary of Energy and not its negation: 'The negations must be destroyed to redeem the Contraries.'[5] Religion misunderstands these Contraries, downgrading them into Negations which remain distinct and irredeemable: 'Without Contraries is no progression, Attraction and Repulsion, Reason and Energy, Love and Hate, are necessary to Human Existence.'[6] However: 'From these Contraries spring what the religious call Good and Evil. Good is the passive that obeys Reason. Evil is the active springing from Energy. Good is Heaven. Evil is Hell.'[7] This downgrading of Reason and Energy into divisive Negations is Milton's mistake. In 'The Marriage of Heaven and Hell' Blake writes:

Those who restrain desire do so because theirs is weak enough to be restrained; and the restrainer or reason usurps its place & governs the unwilling. And being restrain'd, it by degrees becomes passive, till it is only the shadow of desire. The history of this is written in *Paradise Lost*, & the Governor or Reason is call'd Messiah. And the original Archangel or possessor of the command of the heavenly host, is call'd the Devil or Satan, and his children are call'd Sin & Death. But in the Book of Job, Milton's Messiah is call'd Satan. For this history has been adopted by both parties. It indeed appear'd to Reason as if Desire was cast out; but the Devil's account is, that the Messiah fell & formed a heaven of what he stole from the abyss.

This is shown in the Gospel, where he prays to the father to send the comforter, or Desire, that Reason may have Ideas to build on; the Jehovah of the Bible being no other than he who dwells in flaming fire. Know that after Christ's death, he became Jehovah. But in Milton, the Father is Destiny, the Son a Ratio of the five senses, & the holy-Ghost Vacuum! Note: The reason Milton wrote in fetters when he Wrote of Angels and of God, and at liberty when of Devils and Hell, is because he was a true Poet and of the Devil's party without knowing it.[8]

Those whose Desire is weak enough to be restrained will be readily controlled by Reason – a Reason of abstract notions divorced from their objects – a Reason which 'usurps its place & governs'.[9] Plato's organisation of the three parts of the soul has been turned upside down. Now it is not Energy that combines with Reason to overcome appetite or Desire but Energy and

Desire that combine to overcome Reason. But all this is seen through a set of irreconcilable opposites. The stunning criticism of Milton is that he unconsciously sided with Energy against Reason. Thus his work is more powerful, more poetic, when he writes of the Devil and of Hell than of the angels and of God. Milton is on the right side but nonetheless on *one* side of a dualism, on one side of two warring Negations.

In 'The Marriage of Heaven and Hell' true Energy which delights in the form of true Reason is seen by Blake as confined and restricted by the Ratio – 'mental Dieties'[10] – abstracted from their objects. This separation of abstract ideas from the objects of which they are the ideas is the work of 'Priesthood'[11] which then: 'pronounc'd that the Gods had order'd such things';[12] and, 'Thus men forgot that All deities reside in the human breast'.[13] Having once forgotten this vital knowledge, Priesthood could label it blasphemy, attribute it to the Devil and establish the rule of Reason over Energy – of good over evil.

Yet Blake, too, retreated from this knowledge and set himself up against Priesthood, seeing it as the destroyer of human potential, the denier of the truth that deities are not abstracted 'Nobodaddies'[14] but are beings which 'reside in the human breast', Blake himself believing that the Devil's party which fights against Priesthood is the keeper of true creativity. At this stage Blake saw this fall as personified in Milton, who thought he was writing the great Christian epic but was, in fact, destroying it. In Milton's two great poems the true hero is the Satan of the Book of Job. And Satan is the true Jesus.

Blake saw this polarisation as implying a loss of the imaginative moment in which there is a fusion of the prophet and the artist; that is, of the holy and its expression in the world. Once this vital moment of recognition is dimmed, that part of the artist which speaks prophecy is dislocated from that part which is artist only, and the magic of the spell in which the Imagination is held together is destroyed. Imagination, which is the recognition of the one part by the other, fades. 'The Divine Arts of the Imagination',[15] the expression of Identity, is replaced by the arts of persuasion – the battle to persuade the world to recognise the existence of Imagination. In this way Imagination is transformed into vindication. And the displaying of 'Naked Beauty'[16] which is truth and immediate becomes instead a mediation of the Imagination which is only possible in terms other than its own – in terms of symbolism, theology, metaphysics and mysticism – which are the clothes of beauty and, which, as such, hide its nakedness. A vision that recovers itself, a vision that recalls what has never before been said, becomes merely a process of concealment. What should be both ana-calypse and apo-calypse becomes merely ana-calypse.[17]

In this error which Blake saw in both himself and Milton lies the greatest peril for the poet. For, in the process of vindicating Imagination, imagination itself, 'Naked Beauty', moves into the play of this vindication. Paradoxically, by the very strength of his imaginative powers, the poet is forced to identify Imagination with its display. Blake's art becomes for him the only art. The poet's Selfhood has usurped his Identity – which ought to be the very annihilation of Selfhood.

Blake realised what was happening – that the Selfhood had reasserted itself – and he recognised also that his hero Milton had suffered from the same error, and that this very error was the greatest peril for the creative imagination. Blake, however, began to see something more in this error – that the poet's recognition of this peril is itself the essential clue by which he can be saved, and saved not from it but *by* it. The immediacy of the vision granted by Imagination had been replaced by its vindication, a vindication directed towards a world which could not accept it. Blake, looking for a cause of the need for any such vindication, had picked on Reason (*Urizen*) and accused it of subverting the freedom of creative Imagination. It was Reason that was mediating, putting into a mystical or symbolic framework, the immediacy of the Imagination and not allowing it simply to exist. A duality of Imagination versus Reason had taken the place of the unitary experience which Imagination is. And this duality, which is constantly warring with itself, springs from the Selfhood of the artist.

Reason had appeared unregenerate to Blake exactly because he himself had been unregenerate. He saw that his own selfhood had interposed itself between vision and visionary, or rather was that duality of vision and visionary which allowed them to war one with the other. This duality at war with itself is the greatest peril for the poet. *It is also what saves him from the peril*. Lying at the core of mere vindication is the possibility of letting Imagination stand where it is; that is, of recognising that the duality is itself the

Selfhood that has to be annihilated. Within the struggle between Reason and Energy, at its very centre, lies the recognition that both are elements of that Selfhood which has to be annihilated in order that a regeneration of Identity, of Imagination, can take place. Yet, in this recognition, the poet does not finally overcome the duality and thus end the struggle. *The struggle itself is his creativity.* Or, *regeneration is Imagination.* The regeneration of Identity from Selfhood by the annihilation of Self is the collapsing into each other of the warring elements of Selfhood – Reason and Energy. The Identity of their common ground, of the ground from which they spring, of the intimacy without which no struggle can take place, is itself the poet's Identity. Such a struggle is the way that what belongs together differs.[18] Regeneration is a constant and never-ending struggle, and the poet's high responsibility is to live within it and uncover the hidden moment in which they touch each other and are regenerated.

All this can be put in another way.

In 'The Marriage of Heaven and Hell' Blake had taken the warring of Energy and Reason to be the struggle of the Self against the not-Self, a conflict which could only be resolved by the annihilation of Reason and the victory of Energy – the poetic vision. Later he came to see that this struggle takes place *within* the Self – that it is a struggle of the Self with the non-Self. Blake, seeing this as the struggle that the poet has with himself, has to accept that the poet who allows this struggle to dominate is totally absorbed by his own Selfhood. Negation is divided against Negation. Neither can accept any principle beyond itself and battles to dominate and exclude the other. A Self divided against its Self is the form of Selfhood. But from within the dislocation which this division represents for the poet springs the saviour which, in Blake's vision, is Jesus. Satan, the hermaphrodite, dualistic Selfhood at war with itself now stands in a new struggle over against Jesus. Jesus, divine Identity, springs out of the struggle within the duality of Self by the recognition in each Negation that it itself is the cause of what is hateful in the other. In this way each Negation is transformed into a Contrary. Contraries do not exclude each other. They need each other. They resolve into each other's field of gravity. They circle in each other's spell. 'The synthetic power of Imagination reveals itself in the reconciliation of opposite or discordant qualities.'[19]

The acceptance of the interdependence of the two permits of their being regenerated. 'Without Contraries is no progression'.[20]

Art is Self-annihilation, is the collapsing into each other of the Contraries. Art is the regeneration, the eternal recurrence, of the struggle without which Self-annihilation, creation, cannot occur. Imagination is Self-annihilation. That which saves the poet from the peril of Self, which generates its own Contrary, is the saviour – Jesus. There is a 'Moment in each Day which Satan cannot find' which 'renovates every moment' of the day if 'rightly placed'.[21] This is the 'Void Outside of Existence, which if enter'd into Becomes a womb',[22] a womb which reveals the peril to the poet and allows a regeneration. It is the womb in which inspiration is born, the womb of language in which the poet goes down to the 'Eternal Death'[23] which is spiritual resurrection: 'by Self-annihilation back returning to Life Eternal',[24] which is always the potential of each Self lost in the world of generation. For 'The Imagination is not a State: It is the Human Existence itself',[25] inasmuch as 'God only Acts & Is, in existing Beings or Men.[26]

In travelling this path of eternal regeneration Blake had identified himself with Milton. As early as 'The Marriage of Heaven and Earth' Blake had seen that Milton, perhaps unconsciously, had made Satan the real poetic hero of his two epics. Milton's creative Energy was more inspired when writing of the Devil and of Hell because, as we have seen, he was 'of the Devil's party without knowing it'.[27] Although apparently siding with the power of Reason his real allegiance had lain with the eternal delight of Energy. In the regeneration of Milton's Satan, Blake had found the most personal way of expresing his poetic knowledge at the time of the 'Marriage'. For Blake, Milton's Satan was Messiah, the Saviour, and Milton's Jehovah was the Devil; Heaven was seen in Hell and Hell in Heaven. Thus transposed they could come to a regeneration of each other and a marriage take place.

But by the time of the composition of 'Milton' Blake had travelled some way further along the path of regeneration. The marriage of Heaven and Hell, he could now see, was nothing more than the marriage of one Self to another Self, each of which was at war with the other and thus each of which was in Hell. Not only was Milton's Jehovah the Satan of the Book of Job but Milton's Satan was that Satan also. Blake, inevitably, now called on Milton himself to speak this new knowledge. Identifying himself with Milton, Blake had to accept two things. First that in the marriage of Heaven and Hell, of Energy and Reason, he had been his own Satan; secondly, that Satan was his own Selfhood, one which must be annihilated in order to overcome the Negations, to overcome the struggle between Energy and Reason, Satan and Jehovah. Blake/Milton must come to know his own hermaphrodite duality.

At the opening of 'Milton' the poet Milton dwells in eternity while his Emanation – the six-fold Miltonic female (his three wives and three daughters) – and his Spectre (Satan) dwell in the world of Memory or generation: 'What do I here before the Judgement? Without my Emanation? With the daughters of memory & not with the daughters of inspiration?'[28] He must go down to the World of Memory so as to be united with his Spectre and thus also with his imagination: 'I will go down to Self-annihilation and eternal death, lest the Last Judgement come & find me unannihilate and I be seiz'd & given into the hands of my own Selfhood.'[29] Milton goes down into the World of Memory in the hope of 'by Self-annihilation back returning To life Eternal',[30] to the life of the Imagination which alone exists and through which alone all things truly exist. 'All Things Exist in the Human Imagination';[31] 'Where is Existence Out of Mind or Thought?'[32] Life Eternal, the immediate, is uncovered by the willing annihilation of Self, which can only occur within the play of the Contraries. In this loving acceptance of Self-annihilation, within the struggling interplay, the spell of the Contraries, the Eternal Moment, is touched and prophecy is possible. The poet who, even for an instant, claims the power to speak, who claims power over the prophetic word, will annihilate the power of the word itself to speak prophetically and show itself from within the struggle. Any such claim is made from one or other pole of two indifferent negations. Yet 'The Negation must be destroyed to redeem the Contraries.'[33] Within the struggle of the Contraries the word collapses into the Identity that has annihilated its selfhood: 'she . . . fled into the depths of Milton's shadow as a dove upon the stormy sea'[34] and Prophecy is freed to show itself. Thus Blake's Milton says: 'To bathe in the Waters of Life; to wash off the Not-Human, I come in Self-annihilation & the grandeur of inspiration.'[35]

Such Inspiration speaks itself within the eternal Moment of

Imagination and is seen, on waking, to be truth, 'whether it existed before or not'.[36] This is the very nature of Prophecy. Blake writes from 'Immediate dictation ... without Premeditation & even aainst [his] Will'.[37] When the Bard is asked, 'Where hadst thou this terrible song?', he replies: 'I am inspired; I know it is truth, for I sing according to the inspiration of the poetic genius, who is the eternal all-protecting Divine Humanity.'[38]

As art is Imagination, so Christianity is Art. Art is the creation of abundant Imagination. Imagination creates reality. 'Even as man imagines himself to be, such he is.'[39] Without Imagination God is not – he becomes a mere figure of authority or the justification of dogma – 'Nobodaddy'.[40] For Blake, Christ is God's attempt to attain to man's visionary Imagination and it is in the bodily, sexual, human Christ that this attempt is realised. 'God becomes as we are that we may be as he is.'[41] Imagination is 'the Divine Humanity'.[42] Only when man becomes truly what he is can God become truly what he is. In imagination the body of man is 'the Divine Body [of] ... Jesus [and] ... we are his members'.[43] Thus, 'A Poet, A Painter, A Musician, An Architect: The Man or Woman who is not one of these is not a Christian.'[44] Within an Imaginative Generation, within the spell of the bodily, sexual generation lies the regeneration of imaginative joy: 'O holy Generation, Image of regeneration! O point of mutual forgiveness between Enemies! Birthplace of the Lamb of God incomprehensible.'[45]

Nietzsche

Like Blake in 1788–93, Nietzsche in 1870–1 was establishing for himself the relation between Energy and Reason – the Dionysian and the Apollonian. In *The Birth of Tragedy*, Nietzsche differentiates between dream and intoxication. Dream is clear, the delight of illusion. Imagination produces a clear image of reality; a reflexion of the real. In the Dionysian rite 'nature itself, long alienated and subjugated, rises again to celebrate the reconciliation with her prodigal son, man'.[46] The Energy of music, which is imageless, dwells within the terror and nausea of existence.

But, unlike for Blake, the Dionysian is will-less. Nietzsche realises that no action of his can alter the eternal condition of things, the chaotic suffering of becoming. It is in the Apollonian that action makes sense – if only the sense of illusion. Action requires illusion and it is for this that Apollo created the gods, himself being the appropriate god. 'The gods justified human life by living it themselves',[47] but the life that they justify is Apollonian illusion, whereas life itself remains in the realm of becoming, of cause and effect. Art, tragedy, is the marriage of the one with the other. It is 'an Apollonian embodiment of Dionysian insights and powers'.[48] The Apollonian artist dreams intoxication and makes it god-like.

When, however, the Apollonian loses its contact with the nauseous suffering of existence, reason takes over from art. Plot, action, structure, the discreet world of illusion, takes over from the vortex of creativity. For Nietzsche, Socrates mystified Western art and killed tragedy. For Socrates, the daimonion always acted against irrational judgement; its voice was always one which dissuaded. The roles of Apollo and Dionysus are thus reversed; 'instinct is the critic, consciousness the creator. Truly a monstrosity.'[49] It is this inverted thesis which has ruled in Western culture since the time of Socrates who, 'unable to look with any pleasure into the Dionysian abysses', turned his 'Cyclops' eye – that eye which never glowed with the artist's divine frenzy'[50] – upon tragedy and killed it. Socrates is '*theoretical man*', the man of the 'I will and I can',[51] who accepts 'the illusion that thought, guided by the thread of causation, might plumb the farthest abysses of being and even *correct* it'.[52] This is the metaphysical illusion that produced a whole series of philosophies which are absorbed into what is called 'The History of Metaphysics'. This is why Socrates was happy to die. He had suffused the abysses of existence with metaphysical illusion.

Thus, for Nietzsche as much as for Blake, Dionysus/Desire had first of all to reclaim Will/Energy from the realm of the gods and the metaphysical and drag philosophy back down again to the sphere of human existence. It had to appropriate will from where it was enthroned with Reason and aid Desire in its usurpation of Reason's empire and reestablish tragedy in the modern world.

Once Reason/the Apollonian can escape from its Dionysian ground, history can become process and man is free to develop. Yet this 'freedom' is circumscribed by the very rationality which attracted it. It is a freedom to limit itself, a freedom to accept the dogmatic and customary. It is the freedom of habit, 'a great deadener'.[53] In this freedom men 'acquiesce, . . . their hearts imitate and . . . he who obeys *does not listen to himself*'.[54] There are thus a plurality of moralities to suit specific races, peoples, etc., and one morality is set against another. Each group reserves to itself universality under the divine, and such right action under God is set off against evil.

● Socratic or Judeo-Christian man has used his 'freedom' to reject will and sublimate Energy. The 'herd-man . . . glorifies the qualities through which he is tame'.[55] He has freely chosen to retreat behind a protective wall. His is a willing rejection of will justified by an illusion of the transcendent, of Nobodaddy.[56]

This will is reappropriated by the slave who, recognising his submission to the realm of becoming, throws himself vehemently against it, refusing any longer to pretend that he wills in freedom. Turning against the other, he takes revenge to compensate for his resentment.[57] This is the morality of the Self that overcomes the other, that 'from the outset says No to what is "outside", what is "different", what is "not itself", and *this* No is its creative deed'.[58] Nausea, suffering, existence reasserts itself against becoming in order to save itself from submission – a reassertion which is always a 'reaction' against a 'hostile external world'. Without this inspiration it cannot act at all.[59]

The art of the slave is likewise an escape route from the hostile external and eternal flux of becoming into the Platonic, Apollonian, Christian world of Being. Here, art is the saviour which redeems from the absurdity of existence. It is an 'art of metaphysical solace'.[60] The slave's flight from the hostile realities of becoming into the illusions of Being is opposed to the mastery of suffering in a duality of Negations – on *one* side of which Nietzsche comes down. He is for the Dionysian and against Apollo, for the early tragedies of Sophocles and Aeschylus and against their Apollonian transformation by Socrates and Euripides.

But here Nietzsche himself becomes a slave to his own presentation. He is reacting against what he sees as a false will springing from what is weak, Christian and feminine. This 'will' is not an overcoming of Self but a Self which overcomes an other – an antagonism which overcomes any possible reconciliation, which reasserts itself in the face of the world. The tone of much of Nietzsche's work up to *Zarathustra* and beyond is a pernicious sarcasm directed against what he takes to be a Schopenhauerian 'resignationism' which takes all 'art, heroism, genius, beauty, grand sympathy, knowledge, the will to truth, tragedy' to be a denial of the 'will', to be, in a word, 'the greatest piece of psychological false coinage in history, Christianity alone excepted'.[61]

Nietzsche inverts this Apollonian into a Dionysian priority and, as Blake does, places Energy over Reason. This energy justifies itself as one pole of the dualism. Here, reconciliation is taken to be a submission of will, a sign of weakness against which the single one (*Einzelne*) must rebel in order to realise himself, to raise himself above the beasts. A positive action involving the will is what counts: to be a yes-sayer,[62] to dedicate oneself to 'the vast and boundless declaration of Yes and Amen',[63] even if this means '*negating and destroying*', which are the conditions of saying Yes.[64] 'I obey my Dionysiac nature, which does not know how to separate doing No from saying Yes.'[65] Error is cowardice. In *Macbeth*, error is neutralised by Energy: in spite of all his grotesquely evil deeds, we admire him to the end.[66] Now nihilism has become yes-saying, and philosophy vindication.

Such a will redeems the past in the future. The noble man 'shall not gaze backward but *outward*. You shall love your children's land. Let this love be your new nobility. . . . I bid you set sail and seek it. *Thus* you shall redeem all that is past'.[67] Willing creates. Effect follows cause. Because the gods create good and evil by an act of will, the noble man, in order to retain effective will, is lured away from them for, after all, 'What could one create if gods were there?'[68]

Here expression of Identity has become the art of persuasion and Imagination has been turned into vindication. Dionysian Energy vindicates itself against the Apollonian illusion of Being which is precisely an idealization of the Energy that must stand up to any sign of weakness. Nietzsche has created a 'pathos of distance'[69] which relies on differences between – a pair of Negations at war with each other. Thus Imagination becomes vindication. 'It seeks its opposite only so as to affirm itself more gratefully and triumphantly.'[70]

Parallel to this antagonism of two warring Negations runs the recognition *that this very warring itself is what has to be overcome* or rather, that will has to overcome itself in a Self-overcoming. It must will even more powerfully not what-is-not, in order to effect a change, but exactly what is; not a self overcoming but a Self-overcoming – a non-reactive reflexive that wills what is always already effected, what has always already been willed. This is a recognition that being is merely the horizon of becoming and that, as such, the power to will it must recur eternally, must be an eternal Self-overcoming. And such is Imagination – a redemption in which the Negations become Contraries and are redeemed. Such a redemption for the artist is creativity, a creativity which is not an act of will which changes nature, which imposes itself on nature, but a recognition that it is exactly this effective will which must be overcome in an act of affirmation. Such an affirmation is a redemption in which will attains a potency without weakening, in which the feeling of strength (*Kraftgefühl*) is redirected beyond linear time. It is a will 'without foresight'.[71] It is a will that wills its own existence. Such will wills what was. It craves nothing more fervently than what will have been, to 'redeem by creating all that *was past*'.[72] 'All "it was" is a fragment, a riddle, a dreadful chance, until the creative will says to it, "But I willed it thus", until the creative will says to it "But I will it thus, thus shall I will it."'[73] 'Men must endure their going hence even as their coming hither.'[74] Means of enduring it: the revaluation of all values, no longer joy in certainty but in uncertainty, no longer 'cause and effect', but the continually creative, no longer will to preservation but will to power, no longer the humble expression 'everything is merely subjective', but 'it is also our work – let us be proud of it!'[75] *Amor fati*, Nietzsche calls it. 'Ripeness is all.'[76]

Imagination, redeeming the warring opposites, is prophetic in this sense – it creates what will have been by destroying the Negations in order to redeem the Contraries, 'to compose into one and bring together what is fragment and riddle and dreadful accident'.[77] What is willed here is not an overcoming of fate through strength but the strength to acknowledge fate, to redeem suffering. Creativity is this redemption of what *is*. Creativity is not some cause of which the effect is art but is original; that is, a willing of 'something higher than any reconciliation',[78] a 'will to beget' which is 'unguilty'.[79]

The artist does not represent, does not create beautiful copies of the world. Rather, he or she creates the world through prophecy, through an involuntary willing of eternal recurrence. 'One has no longer any notion of what is an image or a metaphor.'[80] This 'involuntariness of image and metaphor is strangest of all. . . .

Here the words and word-shrines of all being open up before you, here all being wishes to become word, all becoming wishes to learn from you how to speak.'[81]

Creativity is prophecy and is 'the closest *approximation of a world of Becoming to a world of Being*'.[82] 'To impose upon Becoming the character of Being – that is the supreme will to power.'[83] 'The soul that, having Being, dives into Becoming . . . the soul . . . in which all things have their sweep and countersweep and ebb and flood',[84] this soul that wants Becoming, 'that *has* and yet *wants* to want and will . . . is the concept of Dionysus himself'.[85] This spirit who accepts tragedy, 'who bears the heaviest fate . . . can nevertheless be the lightest and most transcendent. . . . [He] who has thought "the most abysmal idea" considers it "one reason more for being himself the eternal Yes to all things"'.[86] A supreme, divine artist recklessly creating and destroying – and this 'is the concept of Dionysus once again'.[87] This is *amor fati*. Or, as Blake would have it, 'God becomes as we are that we may be as he is.'[88] 'A spirit thus emancipated stands in the midst of the universe with a joyful and trusting fatalism, trusting in the fate that only what is separate and individual (*einzeln*) may be rejected, that in the totality everything is redeemed and affirmed. . . . But such a faith is the highest of all possible faiths. I have baptised it with the name of Dionysus.'[89]

Dionysus is the spell of the Contraries, a Self-overcoming by a rebirth which speaks in dithyrambs, the language Zarathustra 'speaks to himself before sunrise'.[90] The Dionysians had occult power and the gift of prophecy, which speaks in dithyrambs. The proper subject of these dithyrambs is the birth of Dionysus, the only god created in a double birth and the only god received by the priests at Delphi on equal terms with Apollo.

Abbreviations and translations

William Blake

LAEP Longman's Annotated English Poets, edited by W.H. Stevenson, London, Longman, 1971

OSA Oxford Standard Authors, edited by Geoffrey Key, London, Oxford University Press, 1986

Friedrich Nietzsche

Werke, Herausgegeben von Giorgio Collin und Mazzino Montinari, Berlin, Walter de Gruyter, 1970

Beyond Good and Evil, translated by R.J. Hollingdale, Harmondsworth, Middlesex, Penguin Books, 1973

The Birth of Tragedy, translated by Francis Golffing, New York, Doubleday Anchor, 1956

Daybreak, translated by R.J. Hollingdale, Cambridge, Cambridge University Press, 1982

Ecce Homo, translated by Walter Kaufmann, New York, Vintage Books, 1969

The Gay Science, translated by Walter Kaufmann, New York, Vintage Books, 1974

On the Genealogy of Morals, translated by Walter Kaufmann, New York, Vintage Books, 1969

Thus Spoke Zarathustra, translated by R.J. Hollingdale, Harmondsworth, Middlesex, Penguin Books, 1969

Twilight of the Idols, translated by R.J. Hollingdale, Harmondsworth, Middlesex, Penguin Books, 1968

The Will to Power, translated by Walter Kaufmann and R.J. Hollingdale, New York, Random House, 1967

Notes

Blake

1 Blake, 'Marriage of Heaven and Hell', Plate 4, *OSA 533*, *LAEP 105*
2 Ibid.
3 Ibid.
4 Ibid.

5 Blake, 'Milton', Bk 2, Plate 40:34, *OSA* 533, *LAEP* 563
6 Blake, 'Marriage of Heaven and Hell', Plate 3, *OSA* 149, *LAEP* 105
7 Ibid.
8 Blake, 'Marriage of Heaven and Hell', Plates 5–6, *OSA* 149–50, *LAEP* 106–7
9 Ibid.
10 Blake, 'Marriage of Heaven and Hell', Plate 11, *OSA* 153, *LAEP* 111
11 Ibid.
12 Ibid.
13 Ibid.
14 Blake, 'To Nobodaddy', poem in the 1791–2 notebook, *OSA* 171, *LAEP* 155
15 Blake, 'Jerusalem', Chapter 4, Plate 77, Intro, *OSA* 716–7, *LAEP* 794
16 Blake, 'Milton', Book 1, Plate 4:29, *OSA* 484, *LAEP* 569
17 S.T. Coleridge, Letter to H.F. Cary of 6 February 1818 in *Collected Letters of S.T. Coleridge*, edited by E.L. Griggs, Oxford, Clarendon Press, 1959, Vol IV p.1114
18 Martin Heidegger, ' . . . *dicterisch wohnet der mensch* . . . ' in *Vorträge und Aufsätze*, Neske, 1967, Vol 11 p.67, translated by A. Hofstadter, as ' . . . poetically man dwells . . . ' in *Poetry, Language, Thought*, Harper and Row, 1971, p.218–9
19 S.T. Coleridge, 'Principles of Genial Criticism', addenda to the *Biographia Literaria*, London, Rest Fenner, 1817, Vol II p.245
20 Blake, 'Marriage of Heaven and Hell', Plate 3, *OSA* 149, *LAEP* 10
21 Blake, 'Milton', Book 2, Plate 35:42, *OSA* 526, *LAEP* 550
22 Blake, 'Milton', Book 2, Plate 41:37–42:1, *OSA* 534, *LAEP* 564
23 Blake, 'Milton', Book 2, Plate 42:2, *OSA* 534, *LAEP* 564
24 Blake, 'Vala' or 'The Four Zoas', Night 7a:344–5, *OSA* 328, 340–1, *LAEP* 384
25 Blake, 'Milton', Additional Plate 32:32, *OSA* 522, *LAEP* 574
26 Blake, 'Marriage of Heaven and Hell', Plate 16, *OSA* 155, *LAEP* 115
27 Blake, 'Marriage of Heaven and Hell', Plates 5–6, *OSA* 150, *LAEP* 107
28 Blake, 'Milton', Bk 1, Plate 14:28–9, *OSA* 495–6, *LAEP* 505
29 Blake, 'Milton', Bk 1, Plate 14:22–4, *OSA* 495, *LAEP* 505
30 Blake, 'Vala' or 'The Four Zoas', Night 7a:344–5, *OSA* 328, 340–1, *LAEP* 384
31 Blake, 'Jerusalem', Chapter 3, Plate 69:25, *OSA* 707, *LAEP* 777
32 Blake, 'A Vison of the Last Judgement' – final paragraph, *OSA* 617
33 Blake, 'Milton', Bk 2, Plate 40:33, *OSA* 533, *LAEP* 563
34 Blake, 'Milton', Bk 2, Plate 42:5–6, *OSA* 534, *LAEP* 534
35 Blake, 'Milton', Bk 2, Plate 41:1–2, *OSA* 533, *LAEP* 563
36 Keats, Letter to Benjamin Bailey of 22 November 1817
37 Blake, Letter to Thomas Butts of 25 April 1803 in *The Letters of William Blake*, Oxford, The Clarendon Press, 1980, p.55, also *OSA* 823

38 Blake, 'Milton', Plate 13:50, *OSA* 495, *LAEP* 504
39 Blake, 'A Vision of the Last Judgement', plate 80, *OSA* 823
40 Blake, 'To Nobodaddy', poem in the 1791–2 notebook, *OSA* 171
41 Blake, 'There is No Natural Religion', Second Series, *OSA* 98
42 Blake, 'Jerusalem', Chapter 3, Plate 70:19–20, *OSA* 709, *LAEP* 779
43 Blake, 'The Laocoon', *OSA* 766
44 Ibid.
45 Blake, 'Jerusalem', Chapter 1, Plate 7:65–7, *OSA* 626, *LAEP* 640

Nietzsche

46 *GT* 1, *Werke*, Vol. III:1, p.25, trans. p.23
47 *GT* 3, *Werke*, Vol. III:1 p.32, trans. p.30
48 *GT* 8, *Werke*, Vol. III:1, p.58, trans. p.57
49 or 'a truly monstrous defect' '*wahre monstrositat per defectum*', *GT* 13, *Werke*, Vol. III:1, p.86, trans. pp.84–5
50 *GT* 14 *Werke*, Vol. III:1, p.88, trans. p.86
51 *GT* 15 *Werke*, Vol. III:1, p.94, trans. p.92
52 *GT* 15 *Werke*, Vol. III:1, p.95, trans. p.93
53 Samuel Beckett, *Waiting for Godot*, London, Faber and Faber, 1965, p.91
54 *ASZ* III:12, '*Von alten und neuen Tafeln*' ('Of Old and New Law Tables') s. 7, *Werke*, Vol. VI:1, p.247, trans. p.218
55 *JGB*, *Werke*, Vol. VA:2, p.122, trans. p.102
56 Blake, 'To Nobodaddy' *OSA* 171, *LAEP* 155; see Ortega y Gasset, *Unas Lecciones de Metafisica* in *Obras Completas*, Madrid, Revista de Occidente, 1966, Vol. IV, p.219, translated by M. Adams, *Some Lessons in Metaphysics*, Norton, New York, 1969, pp.15–16
57 *GM*, Essay 1:10 *Werke*, Vol. VI:2, p.284–8, trans. p.36–8
58 Ibid. *Werke*, Vol. VI:2, p.284–5, trans. p.36
59 Ibid. *Werke*, Vol. VI:2, p.285, trans. p.37
60 *GT*, Intro. 7, *Werke*, Vol. III:1, p.16, trans. p.14
61 *GD* 21, *Werke*, Vol. VI:3, p.119, trans. p.80
62 *FW* Bk 4, s. 276, *Werke*, Vol. V:2, p.201, trans. p.233 and '*Die Sieben Seigel*' (*Das Ja-und Amen-Lied*) in *ASZ* III, s. 16, *Werke*, Vol. VI:1, p.283, trans. p.244 passim
63 *ASZ* III:4, '*Vor Sonnen-Aufgang*' ('Before Sunrise'), *Werke*, Vol. VI:1, p.204, trans. p.185
64 *EH*: '*Warum ich ein Schicsal bin*' ('Why I am a Destiny'), s.4, *Werke*, Vol. VI:3, p.366, trans. p.328
65 Ibid., *Werke*, Vol. VI:3, p.364, trans. p.327
66 *M*, Bk4, s.240, *Werke*, Vol. V:1, p.203–4, trans. p.140–1
67 *ASZ* III:12, '*Von alten und neuen Tafeln*' ('Of Old and New Tables'), s. 12 *Werke*, Vol. VI:1, p.251, trans. p.221
68 *EH*, *ASZ*:8, *Werke*, Vol. VI:3, p.347, trans. p.309

69 *JGB* 257, *Werke*, Vol. III, p.173, trans. p.173
70 *GM*, Essay 1:10, *Werke*, Vol. III: 228, trans. p.37
71 *ASZ* II:21, '*Von der Menschen Klugheit*' ('Of Manly Prudence'), *Werke*, Vol. VI:1, p.180, trans. p.164
72 *ASZ* III:12, '*Von alten und neuen Tafeln*' ('Of Old and New Tables'), s.3, *Werke*, Vol. VI:1, p.245, trans. p.216
73 *ASZ* II:20, '*Von der Erlösung*' ('Of Redemption'), *Werke*, Vol. VI:1, p.177, trans. p.163
74 Shakespeare, *King Lear*, Act V, sc. ii, line 11
75 *WM* s.26 [284], *Werke* Vol. VII:2, p.223; trans. s.1059, p.545
76 Shakespeare, *King Lear*, Act V sc. ii, line 11
77 *ASZ* II:20, '*Von der Erlosung*' ('Of Redemption'), *Werke*, Vol. VI:1, p.175, trans. p.161; also see *EH*, *ASZ*:8, *Werke*, Vol. VI:3, p.346, trans. p.308
78 Ibid. *Werke*, Vol. VI:1, p.177, trans. p.163
79 *EH ASZ*:8, *Werke*, Vol. VI:3, p.346, trans. p.309
80 *EH ASZ*:3, *Werke*, Vol. VI:3, p.338, trans. pp.300–1
81 Ibid. *Werke*, Vol. VI:3, p.338, trans. p.301
82 *WM*, s.7 [54], *Werke*, Vol. VII:2, p.320, trans. s.617, p.330
83 Idem.
84 *EH ASZ*:6, *Werke*, Vol. VI:3, p.342, trans. p.305–6
85 Idem.
86 Ibid. *Werke*, Vol. VI:3, p.343, trans. p.306
87 Idem.
88 Blake, 'There is No Natural Religion', Second Series. Application *OSA* 97
89 *EH ASZ*:6, *Werke*, Vol. VI:3, p.342, trans. p.305
90 *EH ASZ*:7, *Werke*, Vol. VI:3, p.343, trans. p.306

· 5 ·

Consultations with the Paternal Shadow: Gasché, Derrida and Klossowski on Ecce Homo.

DAVID FARRELL KRELL

In memory of the Little Joseph Nietzsche, 1848–1850

Ecce Homo – an autobiography? At all events, a tale of fathers and mothers, loves and execrations. And a series of riddles in and about the text. For example, the riddle of an entire section – the third section of Part One, 'Why I Am So Wise' – that only recently has been restored to the form that Nietzsche himself, on the eve of his collapse, devised for it. My question is whether this textual riddle (or confusion) affects three otherwise compelling interpretations of *Ecce Homo*, those of Rodolphe Gasché, Jacques Derrida, and Pierre Klossowski.[1]

On 29 December 1888, from Turin, Nietzsche mailed to his publisher G.C. Naumann a large packet of corrections for the manuscript of *Ecce Homo*. Among them was an entirely recast section three of Part One, which Nietzsche instructed Naumann to insert in place of the one then in his possession. The revised section came to light in July of 1969 among the papers of Heinrich Köselitz (Peter Gast) in the Nietzsche collection of the Goethe-Schiller Archive in Weimar. Köselitz had made a careful copy of Nietzsche's original, which Naumann had passed on to him, before sending that original to Nietzsche's mother and sister – who promptly destroyed it. The first version of *Ecce Homo*, I, 3, written in October of 1888 and present in most editions to date, reads as follows:[2]

Diese doppelte Reihe von Erfahrungen, diese Zugänglichkeit zu anscheinend getrennten Welten wiederholt sich in meiner Natur in jeder Hinsicht – ich bin ein Doppelgänger, ich habe auch das »zweite« Gesicht noch außer dem ersten. *Und* vielleicht auch noch das dritte . . . Schon meiner Abkunft nach ist mir ein Blick erlaubt jenseits aller bloß bloß lokal, national bedingten Perspektiven, es kostet mich keine Mühe, ein »guter Europäer« zu sein. Andrerseits bin ich vielleicht mehr deutsch, als jetzige Deutsche, bloße Reichsdeutsche es noch zu sein vermöchten – ich, der letzte *antipolitische* Deutsche. Und doch waren meine Vorfahren polnische Edelleute: iche habe von daher viel Rassen-Instinkte im Leibe, wer weiß; zuletzt gar noch das *liberum veto*. Denke ich daran, wie oft ich unterwegs als Pole angeredet werde und von Polen selbst, wie selten man mich für einen Deutschen nimmt, so könnte es scheinen, daß ich nur zu den *angesprenkelten* Deutschen gehörte. Aber meine Mutter, Franziska Oehler, ist jedenfalls etwas sehr Deutsches; insgleichen meine Großmutter väterlicherseits, Erdmuthe Krause. Letztere lebte ihre ganze Jugend mitten im guten alten Weimar, nicht ohne Zusammenhang mit dem Goetheschen Kreise. Ihr Bruder, der Professor der Theologie Krause in Königsberg, wurde nach Herders Tod als Generalsuperintendent nach Weimar berufen. Es ist nicht

This double series of experiences, this access to apparently quite disparate worlds, repeats itself in every aspect of my nature – I am an *alter ego*, I also have the 'second' sight [or: the 'second' face: *Gesicht*], in addition to the first. *And* perhaps the third as well. . . . My very lineage grants me a glimpse beyond all merely locally or nationally conditioned perspectives; no great exertion is required for me to be a good European. On the other hand, I am perhaps more German than our contemporary Germans – these mere Imperial Germans – are able to be: – I, the last *antipolitical* German. And yet my ancestors belonged to the Polish aristocracy: who knows, that may be the reason why I incorporate so many instincts pertaining to race, up to and including the liberum veto. When I think how often in my travels I am addressed as though I were a Pole, and by Poles themselves, and how rarely anyone takes me to be a German, it might well seem that I only belonged to the *mottled* Germans. Yet my mother, Franziska Oehler, is at all events a very German phenomenon, as in my paternal grandmother, Erdmuthe Krause. The latter lived throughout her youth in the heart of good old Weimar, and not without a connection to Goethe's circle. Her brother, Professor Krause, a Königsbergian theologian, was appointed General Superintendent in Weimar after Herder's death. It

unmöglich, daß ihre Mutter, meine Urgroßmutter, unter dem Namen »Muthgen« im Tagebuch des jungen Goethe vorkommt. Sie verheiratete sich zum zweiten Mal mit dem Superintendent Nietzsche in Eilenburg; an dem Tage des großen Kriegsjahrs 1813, wo Napoleón mit seinem Generalstab in Eilenburg einzog, am 10. Oktober hatte sie ihre Niederkunft. Sie war, als Sächsin, eine große Verehrerin Napoleons; es könnte sein, daß ich's auch noch bin. Mein Vater, 1813 geboren, starb 1849. Er lebte, bevor er das Pfarramt der Gemeinde Röcken unweit Lützen übernahm, einige Jahre auf dem Altenburger Schlosse und unterrichtete die vier Prinzessinnen daselbst. Seine Schülerinnen sind die Königin von Hannover, die Großfürstin Constantin, die Großherzogin von Oldenburg und die Prinzeß Therese von Sachsen-Altenburg. Er war voll tiefer Pietät gegen den preußischen König Friedrich Wilhelm den Vierten, von dem er auch sein Pfarramt erhielt; die Ereignisse von 1848 betrübten ihn über die Maßen. Ich selber, am Geburtstage des genannten Königs geboren, am 15. Oktober, erheilt, wie billig, die Hohenzollern-Namen *Friedrich* Wilhelm. Einen Vorteil hatte jedenfalls die Wahl dieses Tages: mein Geburtstag war meine ganze Kindheit hindurch ein Festtag. – Ich betrachte es als ein großes Vorrecht, einen solchen Vater gehabt zu haben: es scheint mir sogar, daß sich damit alles erklärt, was ich sonst an Vorrechten habe – das Leben, das große Ja zum Leben *nicht* eingerechnet. Vor allem, daß es für mich keiner Absicht dazu bedarf,

is not impossible that her mother, my great grandmother, appears in the young Goethe's diary under the name 'Muthgen'. She married a second time, taking the hand of Superintendent Nietzsche in Eilenburg; during that vital year in the Napoleonic Wars, 1813, on October 10, the very day Napoleon marched into Eilenburg with his General Staff, she lay in childbirth. Being a Saxon, she was a great admirer of Napoleon's; it may well be that I still am. My father, born in 1813, died in 1949. Before he became pastor of the congregation at Röcken, near Lützen, he lived for several years at Altenburg Castle and tutored the four princesses there. His pupils are now the Queen of Hanover, the Grand Princess Constantina, the Grand Duchess of Oldenburg, and Princess Theres of Saxony-Altenburg. He was full of profound piety toward the Prussian king, Friedrich Wilhelm IV, from whom he had received his pastorate; the events of 1848 troubled him egregiously. I myself, born on the king's birthday, October 15, received, as was fitting, the Hohenzollern name *Friedrich* Wilhelm. In any case, the choice of this day had one advantage: throughout my childhood my birthday was a holiday. – I regard the fact that I had such a father as a great privilege: it even seems to me that this accounts for whatever other privileges I possess – life, the magnificent Yes to life, *not* included. Above all, that I need exercise no special intention, but can simply wait, in order to enter willy nilly into a world of lofty and delicate things: I am at home there,

sondern eines bloßen Abwartens, um unfreiwillig in eine Welt hoher und zarter Dinge einzutreten: ich bin dort zu Hause, meine innerste Leidenschaft wird dort erst frei. Daß ich für dies Vorrecht beinahe mit dem Leben zahlte, ist gewiß kein unbilliger Handel. – Um nur etwas von mienem Zarathustra zu verstehn, muß man vielleicht ähnlich bedingt sein, wie ich es bin – mit einem Fuße *jenseits* des Lebens . . .

my innermost passion is liberated there alone. That I paid for this privilege almost with my life is, to be sure, no petty exchange. – In order to understand anything at all of my *Zarathustra*, one must perhaps be conditioned in a way similar to the way I am – with one foot *beyond* life.

Nietzsche's revised text, obliterated by his mother and/or sister but preserved by Köselitz, reads as follows:[3]

Ich betrachte es als ein grosses Vorrecht, einen solchen Vater gehabt zu haben: die Bauern, vor denen er predigte – denn er war, nachdem er einige Jahre am Altenburger Hofe gelebt hatte, die letzten Jahre Prediger – sagten, so müsse wohl ein Engel aussehn. – Und heirmit berühre ich die Frage der Rasse. Ich bin ein polnischer Edelmann pur sang, dem auch nicht ein Tropfen schlechtes Blut beigemischt ist, am wenigsten deutsches. Wenn ich den tiefsten Gegensatz zu mir suche, die unausrechenbare Gemeinheit der Instinkte, so finde ich immer meine Mutter und Schwester, – mit solcher canaille mich verwandt zu glauben wäre eine Lästerung auf meine Göttlichkeit. Die Behandlung, die ich von Seiten meiner Mutter und Schwester erfahre, bis auf diesen Augenblick, flösst mir ein unsägliches Grauen ein: hier arbeitet eine vollkommene Höllenmaschine, mit unfehlbarer Sicherheit über den Augenblick, wo man mich blutig verwunden kann – in meinen höchsten Augenblicken, . . . denn da fehlt

I regard the fact that I had such a father as a great privilege: the peasants to whom he preached – for, during his last years, after having lived for several years at the court of Altenburg, he was a preacher – used to say that the angels must look like him. – And herewith I touch on the question of race. I am a pure-blooded Polish nobleman, in whom not a drop of ignoble blood has been admixed, least of all German blood. Wherever I search for my profoundest opposite, to wit, incalculable vulgarity of instinct, I always find my mother and sister – if I thought I were actually related to such canaille it would be a veritable blasphemy against my divinity. The treatment I have always received from my mother and sister – up to the present moment – fills me with unutterable horror: here a highly perfected, infernal machine is at work, one that operates with unfailing accuracy at the very moment when I am most vulnerable and most likely to bleed – during my supreme moments . . . for in these

jede Kraft, sich gegen giftiges Gewürm zu wehren . . . Die physiologische Contiguität ermöglicht eine solche disharmonia praestabilita . . . Aber ich bekenne, dass der tiefste Einwand gegen die „ewige Wiederkunft", mein eigentlich abgründlicher Gedanke, immer Mutter und Schwester sind. – Aber auch als Pole bin ich ein ungeheurer Atavismus. Man würde Jahrhunderte zurückzugehn haben, um diese vornehmste Rasse, die es auf Erden gab, in dem Masse instinktrein zu finden, wie ich sie darstelle. Ich habe gegen Alles, was heute noblesse heisst, ein souveraines Gefühl von Distinktion, – ich würde dem jungen deutschen Kaiser nicht die Ehre zugestehn, mein Kutscher zu sein. Es giebt einen einzigen Fall, wo ich meines Gleichen anerkenne – ich bekenne es mit tiefer Dankbarkeit. Frau Cosima Wagner ist bei Weitem die vornehmste Natur; und, damit ich kein Wort zu wenig sage, sage ich, dass Richard Wagner der mir bei Weitem verwandteste Mann war . . .Der Rest ist Schweigen . . . Alle herrschenden Begriffe über Verwandtschafts-Grad sind ein physiologischer Widersinn, der nicht überboten werden kann. Der Papst treibt heute noch Handel mit diesem Widersinn. Man ist am wenigsten mit seinen Eltern verwandt: es wäre das äusserste Zeichen von Gemeinheit, seinen Eltern verwandt zu sein. Die höheren Naturen haben ihren Ursprung unendlich weiter zurück, auf sie hin hat am längsten gesammelt, gespart, gehäuft werden müssen. Die grossen

one lacks all the energy that would be needed to defend oneself against venomous vipers. . . . Physiological contiguity makes such a *disharmoni praestabilita* possible. . . . But I confess that the most profound objection to the eternal return, that is, to my properly *abyssal* thought, is always mother and sister. – Yet even as a Pole I am an incredible atavism. One would have to go back centuries in order to find this noblest of races ever to exist on Earth as pristine in its instincts as I exhibit them here and now. Toward everything today that calls itself *noblesse* I possess a sovereign feeling of distinction – I wouldn't do our young Kaiser the honor of appointing him my driver. There is one single case in which I acknowledge my equal – I confess it with profound gratitude. Frau Cosima Wagner is the noblest nature by far; and, in order not to leave a single word unsaid, I say that Richard Wagner was by far the man most akin to me. . . . The rest is silence. All the prevailing concepts that govern degrees of consanguinity are unsurpassable physiological nonsense. Even today the Pope insists on trafficking in such absurdity. One is *least* akin to one's parents. Higher natures have their origins much, much farther back; with a view to these natures, much had to be accumulated, saved, horded. The *greatest* individuals are the oldest: I do not understand it, but Julius Caesar could be my father – *or* Alexander, this Dionysos in the flesh. At the very moment I write this the mail brings me a Dionysos-head.

Individuen sind die ältesten: ich
verstehe es nicht, aber Julius Cäsar
könnte mein Vater sein – oder
Alexander, dieser leibhafte
Dionysos . . . In diesem
Augenblick, wo ich dies schreibe,
bringt die Post mir einen Dionysos-
Kopf.

Ignoring most of the intriguing contrasts between these two
texts, and setting aside Nietzsche's (bogus) claim to aristocratic
Polish ancestry and his (mistaken) grandmotherly liaison with
Goethe, I wish to stress what is perhaps obvious to any first
reading. While the paternal shadow in the revised text still retains
something of its foreboding aspect, it is now essentially benign,
even 'angelic'. To have had such a father – both texts proclaim –
was a 'privilege'. Gone from the revised text, however, are the
romanzas of the Oehler side, the maternal side, of Nietzsche's
family, as well as of that 'very German phenomenon' of the
paternal grandmother, the Krause side. The revised account leaves
us with two profound objections to the eternal recurrence of the
same – who are delighted to act as Nietzsche's editors.

The very first section of *Ecce Homo*, Part One, begins as follows:

The fortune of my existence, perhaps its very singularity, lies in its
fatality: I have – to put it in the form of a riddle – as my father already
died; as my mother I am still alive and am growing old. This double
provenance, from the highest and the lowest rungs on the ladder of life, as
it were, simultaneously *décadent* and *commencement* – this, if anything,
accounts for that neutrality, that freedom from all bias in relation to the
entire problem of life, which perhaps distinguishes me. . . . I know both, I
am both. (6, 264)

Nietzsche's 'riddle', propounded originally as the *conclusion* to
a series of notes we now call the *Ur-Ecce homo* (see 13, 629), is
taken up by Gasché, Derrida and Klossowski in ways that merit
careful attention. All three have meditated on the riddle of
Nietzsche's *double* origin, the non-dialectical, neutral, irreducible
doubling of high and low, ascendancy and decrepitude, mother
and father in Nietzsche's 'life'. However, may the last-named pair
serve as the key to unlock the mystery of the others? Can

we – and does Nietzsche – attribute unequivocally vitality to the mother, enervation and death to the father? Can we assume that it is sheer oversight, or the force of a conventional idiom, that causes him to place 'highest' and 'lowest' in improper sequence, since everywhere else the paternal legacy is listed first? In short, is the *double* provenance ultimately reducible to a *single* binary opposition? Is the riddle so easily riddled?

All three commentators resist such a reduction, though perhaps not always successfully. Indeed, such resistance is difficult. The bulk of *Ecce Homo*, I, 1, emphasizes the fatality for the son of the father's early demise (*Mein Vater starb . . .*), in such a way that the identification of paternity and shadow appears to be a foregone conclusion. Entropy, decline and death: are these not the names and negatives of the father?

However, if décadence appears to be the paternal legacy, the legacy of vitality and *commencement* (*Anfang*) cannot so readily be attributed to the mother. The second section of Part One refers to such vitality, ascribing it not to her but to Nietzsche's own hand:

> For, discounting the fact that I am a décadent, I am also the opposite of one. . . . As *summa summarum* I was healthy, as nook and cranny, as specialty, I was décadent. . . . I took hold of myself [*Ich nahm mich selbst in die Hand*], I made myself healthy again. . . . Out of my will to health, to life, I made my philosophy. . . . – So you see, I am the precise contrary of a décadent. (6, 266–67).

Whether we can take the opposition of *summa summarum* to *Winkel* and *Specialität* as somehow corroborating the equation (mother = life; father = death) is doubtful, unless one insists on identifying the organs that gave Nietzsche particular distress (eyes, brain, and stomach) as those that suffered most from Nietzsche's paternal, spiritual-intellectual heritage. Yet such distress is matched by the anguish induced by that infernal machine of the maternal presbytery. It may well be that much depends on how we read *section 3* of Part One – and on *which version* we read.

In his article, 'Autobiography as Gestalt', Rodolphe Gasché cites these early pages of *Ecce Homo* to which I have been referring. Focussing on Nietzsche's 'double origin', he stresses the philosopher's own search for his 'nethermost self', the self that is to be found nowhere else than *in physiologicis*. Nietzsche's double maternal/paternal face or sight makes him a veritable *Janus bifrons*. Not simply *in physiologicis*, however: Gasché invokes the gateway *Augenblick* in which the eternities of past and future 'affront one another' as an eminent instance of the double structure in Nietzsche's writing. If the gateway – or, as Heidegger would insist, our *standing in* the gateway – closes the ring of eternity in a moment of decision, then the very 'vision' or 'visage' (*Gesicht*) of the gateway marks the closure of infinite past (the dead father) and endless future (the surviving mother).

Although I cannot recount all of Gasché's reading here, I at least want to present his 'first transcription' of the solution to the riddle of Nietzsche's double origin – the 'riddle' here referring, not to the striken shepherd of 'On the Vision and the Riddle', but to Nietzsche's *Ecce Homo*. Gasché writes, with the hand of Nietzsche: 'I have killed myself as my own father so that I can commit incest with myself as my mother while as my father I am preventing myself from being born.' I shall defer discussion of the first half of Gasché's transcription, at once necrological and oedipal, hence oedipal in the full sense (in as much as it would embrace *Oedipus at Colonus*), in order to emphasize the final words: ' . . . while as my father I am preventing myself from being born'. Here the paternal shadow appears as Chronos – Time jamming the mother, as yet untouched by the surgical *legerdemain* of the son. That Nietzsche bore his father with him always, as though he (Nietzsche, Friedrich) were his own mother, filled by the father, pregnant by and with him; that Nietzsche felt himself to be reliving the misfortunes and illnesses of the father, waiting for his own brain to ooze, anticipating his mother's tears, the doctor's tragic mein – who can doubt these things? Nietzsche took his chances with such a father, the *Glück* of his existence, and such chances took him. Unlike the latter case of Jean-Paul Sartre, Nietzsche for the first four years of his life *knew* his father, sat on his lap – and in German a lap is a womb: *Schoß* – at the piano, rapt to his father's improvisations, enthralled by the origins of all music. How could Nietzsche ever have been born from such a lap? Once borne on it, he would never be released, never partured. It is as though in later years his father emerged from the grave to fetch the young son back to his bosom, back to the origins of all music. But that is to anticipate. Indeed, nothing about the paternal shadow seems to follow in good order, generation upon generation; everything seems to anticipate and presuppose a long lineage. On both sides, both sides.

To hear with a new ear the names of Nietzsche, Friedrich Wilhelm, *who is himself dead*, and whose very signature is now a mark of death – that is the task Jacques Derrida assigns himself in '*La logique de la vivante*'. To read with a new eye the 'thanatography' of Nietzsche's 'biography', to take up again the relation of the 'I', writing and death as developed, for example, in chapter seven of *La voix et le phénomène*. Yet the present investigation of the logic of the living is less a logic than a gloss on *Glas*, a logic of the knell, an obsequy. Derrida's is an essay on obsequence. It is Nietzsche's fatality to be both neutral (neither-nor) and doubling (both-and), to be *between* the dead and the living, between *le (père) mort* and *la (mère) vivante*, to be both death, *la mort*, and life, *la vie*, during that stretch of time that he himself, Nietzsche, Friedrich Wilhelm is (was) alive, *le vivant*. Obsequence turns out to be an enigmatic sort of sequentiality, not of generation upon generation, but of multiple and even undecidable first-person existences. Note in the following passage the variety of possible senses and sequences of the *je suis*, 'I am' (*être*) and 'I follow' (*suivre*):

> En tant que *je suis* mon père, je suis mort, je suis le mort et je suis la mort. En tant que *je suis* ma mère, je suis la vie qui persévère, le vivant, la vivante. Je suis mon père, ma mère et moi, mon fils et moi, la mort et la vie, le mort et la vivante, etc.[4]

Derrida's transcription of the riddle thus doubles up on itself in a way that no English transcription can. One attempt to retranscribe Derrida's transcription – to anglicize the logic of obsequence:

> In so far as I *follow* my father, I am dead; I am and follow the dead progenitor, I am and follow death. In so far as I *follow* my mother, I am the life that perseveres [cf., by way of contrast, Lacan: *je*, *père*, *sévère*], I am the living male heir, I am the progenitrix. I am and follow my father, my mother and me, my son and me, death and life, the dead progenitor and the living progenitrix.

Thus Derrida spins out the riddle into a complex fable of death and living-on, *ob-sequence* and *survivance*. And yet there is a tendency in Derrida's fable to identify the father with decadence and to acknowledge the mother, without further ado, as she who survives collapse. Like Ursula in Garcia Marquez's *Cien años de soledad*, Franziska would be she who lives on, she who survives to bury her son.

The son whom Derrida mistakenly calls *le fils unique*. Forgetting Little Joseph.

And even if we are to set Little Joseph aside, we may ask whether the survival of the mother is the *survivance* of life or of deathly obsequ(i)ence.

Pierre Klossowski begins his 'Consultation of the Paternal Shadow' by remarking, apropos of Nietzsche's talent for riddles, that to pose a riddle is 'to simulate a necessity in order to flee the vacuity of something arbitrary'. Nietzsche's own account of the fortune and fatality of his 'double origin', the fable of mother and father, Klossowski therefore calls 'the *shadow* of a solution' to the puzzle of his 'life'. Yet even this shadow is double, multiple, and ultimately undecidable. It is at once the oneiric shadow of the father and the oppressive shadow(s) of the mother-in-mourning and of all the women in the presbytery who raise Little Fritz, *Herzenfritz*.

Why is the paternal shadow 'oneiric'? Klossowski cites two versions of a premonitory dream that Nietzsche had – presumably at five-and-a-half years of age, about eighteen months after his father's death – which foretold the sudden death of his younger brother, Little Joseph, *Josephchen*. The first report, composed at Christmas, 1856, reads as follows:

At that time I once dreamt that I heard the sounds of the church organ, playing as it did during the funeral [i.e. of Nietzsche's father]. When I perceived what lay behind these sounds a gravemound suddenly opened and my father, wrapped in linen cerements, emerged from it. He hurried into the church and returned a moment later with a child in his arms. The tomb yawned again, he entered, and the cover closed over the opening. The sterterous sounds of the organ ceased instantly, and I awoke. On the day that followed this night Little Joseph abruptly fell ill, seized by severe cramps, and after a few hours he died. Our grief knew no bounds. My dream had been fulfilled completely. The tiny corpse was laid to rest in his father's arms.[5]

Note the progression, the obsequence, of this first account: hearing organ music, seeing nothing as yet, discovering that this is the music of the deceased father – not the improvisations played while Little Fritz sat on his father's lap (alone before Josephchen's arrival?) but the music of interment – and then the gaping of the grave. His father hurries into the church and emerges carrying a child, *ein Kind*, in his arms. Not *Herzenfritz*, who is observing all this (but from where? and how? presumably from the second floor of the large country house that looked out over the church and the adjacent cemetery: *Ich bin als Pflanze nahe dem Gottesacker, als Mensch in einem Pfarrhaus geboren* – another doubling here, except that if as a human being Nietzsche was born in a pastor's house, in the house of the father, then his life as a plant is rooted in God's Green Acre, that is, the cemetery, which would be the mother), not Little Fritz but *Little Joseph* is the dead man's object.

This first account, written at age twelve, is followed by a second, composed when Nietzsche was seventeen:

Some months later [i.e., following the death of the father], a second misfortune struck me, a misfortune of which I had a premonition, thanks to a remarkable dream. I felt as though I could hear muffled organ music coming from the nearby church. Surprised, I open the window that looked out over the church and cemetery. My father's grave opens, a white figure emerges and disappears into the church. The gloomy, uncanny sounds continue to surge; the white figure appears again, carrying something under his arm that I did not clearly recognize. The gravemound yawns, the figure sinks into it, the organ goes silent – I waken. The following morning my younger brother, a lively and gifted child, is seized by cramps, and a half-hour later he is dead. He was buried right next to my father's grave.[6]

Klossowski notes several deviations from the first account in the second. The music is now muffled, sinister; the dreamer himself opens a window to seek the source of the music, uncanny yet familiar; the 'thing' borne under the father's arms is now not readily identifiable; and Josephchen (for it *will* be he even if no name is mentioned) is now, after his seizure with cramps, cramps caused perhaps by the tightening of that paternal grasp, removed from his father's arms (*their* father's arms) and buried *alongside*. Klossowski, perhaps recalling chapter four of the Wolfman case, and himself alluding to the 'compensatory value of a reconstitution of the traumatism' (*Beyond the Pleasure Principle*, chapters two and three), writes now with the hand of the dreamer himself:

I *open* the window and *the tomb is opened*: I open the tomb of my father, who then looks for *me* in the church. My dead father searches me out and carries me off because I am trying to see my dead father [or: trying to see my father dead – *à voir mon père mort*]. I am dead, the father of myself, I suppress my self in order to reawaken in the midst of music. My dead father makes me hear the music. (257)

Although he is looking for *me* in the church, the father finds *Josephchen* instead. Little Joseph is not in the house, but has been removed to the church. Who has removed this gay and gifted child to the pale altar? Who has exposed him to the waxen pastor? Klossowski does not raise this question explicitly. Yet if the oedipal situation applies (recall Gasché: 'I have killed myself as my own father so that I can commit incest with myself as my mother . . . '), then it is not only the father but also the second son who must be removed to God's Green Acre: 'Our grief knew no bounds. My dream had been fulfilled completely. The tiny corpse was laid to rest in his father's arms.' Note the sequence, the obsequence, up to the perfunctory close: muffled organ music; surprised, I open the window (the infant Wolfman's eyes open of themselves, says Freud, to the primal scene: it is a matter of attentive, *interested* observation, insists Freud) that looks out onto the cemetery (*Wie lebendig steht noch der Gottesacker vor mir!* exclaims Nietzsche at age fourteen) where I see my father dead. First my father, then Little Joseph. Our grief knew no bounds. Ours. Me 'n Mum's. Unencumbered. My dream had been fulfilled completely. Alone at last.

Yet if the first of Klossowski's consultations appears to conform to the usual (oedipal) view – negative identification with the father as decadence, transgression and guilt – the second consultation (285 ff.) begins to subvert and displace that view. Klossowski stresses the asymmetry and disequilibrium of Nietzsche's 'double origin': the mother simply does not embody 'commencement' in the way the father adumbrates closure. Keeping before him the shadow of the dead father as a kind of shield or amulet, Nietzsche in the course of his life distances himself increasingly from mother and sister, distances himself through his writing, his texts, such as the new text of *Ecce Homo* I, 3, which no mother or sister should ever have seen. Beneath the forced jollity of a later missive (the last) to Franziska Nietzsche, written on December 21, 1888 (*Meine alte Mutter. . . . Dien altes Geschöpf*), in which he assures her that he is by now *ein ungeheuer berühmtes Tier* ('a monstrously renowned beastie'), we hear overtones that resonate quite distinctly in a letter four days later to Franz Overbeck:

This does *not* prevent my sister from writing to me on October 15 [i.e., on Nietzsche's birthday, the halcyon forty-fourth birthday commemorated by the exergue to *Ecce homo*] that I too ought to commence becoming 'renowned'. . . . All the while she calls me 'Darling Fritz', *Herzensfritz*. . . . This has been going on now for seven years![7]

Thus Nietzsche is driven to invert the oedipal situation: he substitutes himself for the mother and the father's daughter in order to become intimate with the father – 'as through being', says Klossowski, *'his own mother'*.[8] Such inversion/subversion will not go unpunished. Nietzsche's 'real' mother and sister, his 'editors', will eventually suffocate him: Klossowski adduces a mordant word on the mother's 'mortal compassion for the convalescent son'. Indeed, mother and sister represent what Deleuze calls 'the second feminine power'.[9] They embody according to Klossowski, 'Life in its most contemptible form', the sluggish worm and viper – counterimages to the serpent of eternal return.

The consequences of such inversion become increasingly radical in Klossowski's own consultations. If the father is detachment from life, if the father – and not the ghostship of woman – is *Distanz*, then he is also the great healthfulness of the revaluation of all values. Magnificent health is the father's, the deceased father of all genealogy. Hence 'the presence of the dead father as an explanation of Nietzsche's struggle with his own fatality'. Klossowski depicts such distance and struggle as Nietzsche's perilous perch on the crest of a wave: from it Nietzsche can descry with 'ultimate lucidity' the fatality against which he will shatter – and yet that very perception marks the onset of inexpungible darkness. In the end, the end(s) of Nietzsche himself, Friedrich Wilhelm, the disequilibrium of all origins is radicalized. It is his destiny to replace (to follow *and* to be) the mother and to insinuate himself with the oneiric shadow of the father – and thus to follow *and* to be his younger brother, Josephchen. The living mother embodies decay of blood, loss of exuberance, end of adventure, the survival of death, death alone; the dead father, more a dream about life than life itself, yet a dream dreamt by at least one of his sons, embodies – if a shade may be said to embody – the very course and flow (the *sens*) of life. Paternal shadow and gaping tomb become a single sign in Nietzsche's destiny: the sign of *Chaos*. The shadow of the mourning mother, mourning her spouse, mourning Little Joseph, mourning Friedrich Wilhelm, is finally dispersed in what Klossowski calls 'automaternity': 'Yet in order to rediscover *life itself*, Nietzsche, in so far as he is his *own mother*, becomes the child anew [*s'enfante à nouveau*] and becomes his own creature.' (260) Hence 'the necessity to be born to himself from himself and thereby his tendency to restore himself to a double presence, feminine and virile.' (274)

And yet this elevation of the paternal shadow and expulsion of the living mother ought to give us pause. Such 'automaternity', such taking-oneself-in-hand: *Wie? Und dies wäre nicht – circulus vitiosus deus?*[10] The apparent restoration of what Klossowski here calls a 'double presence' and (after Deleuze) 'double affirmation' may well be no more than the dream of the 'perfect object', the dream of the metaphysics (and morals) of undifferentiated presence. Such restoration would forget what it most needs to remember, namely, that Nietzsche's great good luck is his fatality. Automaternity fares no better than autobiography.

Ecce Homo – autobiography? automaternity? shadow?

Autobiography doubles up with absences, not presences, and is thanatography. If Nietzsche, Friedrich Wilhelm, is once again with child, is once again himself a child, that child will turn out to be otherwise. It will be Little Joseph. Doubling up. In the end there will be nothing left for these children – Josephchen, Herzensfritz – but fatal consultation with the paternal shadow, fatal embrace of the mother: the riddle of an origin that will never cease doubling, sundering, receding into the infinite distance of all music.

Notes

1 Rodolphe Gasché, 'Autobiography as Gestalt', originally published in *boundary 2*, IX, 3 and X, 1, 1981; this double issue of *boundary 2* has been published as a volume entitled *Why Nietzsche Now?*, edited by Daniel T. O'Hara, Bloomington and London, Indiana University Press, 1985. Jacques Derrida, 'Logique de la vivante', appears in two places. First, in Derrida, *L'orielle de l'autre*, edited by Claude

Levesque and Christie V. McDonald, Montreal, VLB-Editeur, 1982, pp.13–32; second, in Derrida, *Otobiographies: L'enseignement de Nietzsche et la politique du nom propre*, Paris, Editions Galilée, 1984, p.33–69. And Pierrre Klossowski, *Nietzsche et le cercle vicieux*, revised edition, Paris, Mercure de France, 1969, p.251–84.

I regret not having discovered until after this paper was bound for the printer the remarkable text by Philippe Lacoue-Labarthe, 'L'écho du sujet', in *Le sujet de la philosophie*, Paris, Flammarion, 1979, pp.217–303, which is explicitly on the theme of autobiography and music – something that will play a major role in my own more modest efforts here. I would especially like to have been able to reply to 'La clôture maternelle', pp.296–97.

I cite Nietzsche's works from the *Kritische Studienausgabe*, edited by Giorgio Colli and Mazzino Montinari, Berlin and Munich, de Gruyter and DTV, 1980, by volume and page, eg.: 6, 45. Nietzsche's autobiographical sketches, not contained in Colli-Montinari, I cite from the edition by Karl Schlechta, *Werke in drei Bänden*, Munich, Hanser, 1956. The story of the textual confusion of *Ecce Homo* I, 3, is recounted by Mazzino Montinari in *Nietzsche-Studien*, Band 1, 1972, 380–418.

2 I cite the edition by Karl Schlechta, II, 1, 073–74.

3 See 6, 267–69; for further details on the textual history, see *14*, 460–62 and 472–74.

4 In *L'orielle de l'autre*, p.28; in *Otobiographies*, p.62

5 See the Schlechta edition, III, 17

6 See the Schlechta edition, III, 93

7 Nietzsche, *Sämtliche Briefe, Kritische Studienausgabe*, 8 vols, eds. Giorgio Colli and Mazzino Montinari, Berlin and Munich, de Gruyter and Deutscher Taschenbuch Verlag, 1986, *8*, 542–4; 549 (letters 1204 and 1210)

8 In the second session of the 'Double Séance', Derrida (see *La dissémination*, Paris, Seuil, 1972 p.301n.) cites Freud's references to such inversion in the Wolfman case:

> The phantasm of a second birth was thus here an abbreviated and bowdlerized version of phantasms involving homosexual desire. . . . The rending of the veil is analogous to the opening of the eyes, to the opening of the window. . . . To be born of his father . . . to give him a child at the cost of his own virility . . . homosexuality here finds its supreme and most intimate expression.

See Freud, *Studienausgabe*, Frankfurt am Main, Fischer, 1982, VIII, 231.

9 Gilles Deleuze, *Nietzsche et la philosophie*, Paris, Presses Universitaires de France, 1962, pp.24 and 214

10 *JGB*, no.56 (*5*, 75)

· PART TWO ·

WOMEN, MEN AND MACHINES OF WAR

· 6 ·

Orchids and Muscles

ALPHONSO LINGIS

Man is no longer artist, he has become artwork:
the reign of art throughout nature,
to the supreme delight and satisfaction of the Primal-One,
here reveals itself amid frenzied shudderings.
Here is kneaded the noblest clay,
here is hewn the costliest marble: der Mensch.
                                        NIETZSCHE, GT 1

An artist's utility in the service of the ascetic ideal
is therefore the most proper possible form of
the artist's corruption. *Unfortunately, it is also*
the most common form of corruption:
for nothing is more corruptible than an artist.
                                        NIETZSCHE, ZGM III, 25

The body-builders

A cult, certainly, rather than one of the enterprises – that of *mens sana in corpore sano* – which culture can know and integrate. A cult which has its clandestine repairs, its passwords, its initiations, its legends, its rituals, its undeciphered codes. The alerted eye can spot them in the crowds, not, like punks, by the tribal garb and arcane jewelry, but rather by the way neither work nor leisure garb fit their bodies, by the strained fabrics, the pulled seams. If they wear jewelry, they most often do not wear them as embellishments or citations, but as amulets. Sportswear and beachwear, designer-conceived for voyeurist eroticism, pulled tight over their loins like chastity belts. In the bus-stations and sidewalks, in the midst of the streams of the busy and the preoccupied, space warps and strains about them, as though lacking the gravity these sprung arms and ploughshare thighs are made to furrow. The civilized head that looks at them is deviated; it wonders not where they are going, but where you can get with them. The erotic eye, that which scouts the erotogenic terrain in the body of another – not the rolling surfaces of taut cutaneous membrane, but the spongy zone of susceptibility just beneath and the mucous membrane of orifices – is disconcerted to run into packed thongs of drawn muscle. Not muscle that answers to the ungendered resistance of tools and implements, but specifically male and specifically female muscle alignments. One cannot resist feeling the very hardness of these muscles to be the badgering of the glands of lust. Whole anatomies pumped like priapic erections, contracting poses and shifting with held violence from one pose to the next with the vaginal contractions of labor pains. Flaunting in the nose of an antiseptic consumer public leathery rutting odors, gleaming with oils that deviate the hold the inspecting eye fixes on these bodies into the sliding suctions of octopus eros.

Their codes are undeciphered; one does not understand the programming, or the decision-process, that assigns them their hours in cellars full of iron millstones and rudimentary machines. The process that elaborates, selects, and distributes the programming is not in the control-rooms of culture nor even in the science of coaches and trainers; it is rigged up in their own taciturn and superstitious skulls. The unguarded, unwary eyes with which they walk in the frenetic halls of stock-exchanges or in the night of urban jungles do not seem practised in the predatory uses of the sense-organs perfected by the millenia of hunters whose genes we inherit; and, unlike the surveillance a miller maintains on the ox or the waterwheel that turns the millstone, their eyes unfocused on their unrotating wheels of iron seem rather to watch the inward spread of monotonous fatigue and seeping pain. Their arms that handle but poles without fulcrum and wheels that grind nothing are uneconomic, detaching or transforming nothing from the raw or recycled materials of nature and industry. In their handshake we feel no understanding; we feel an indextrous hand that is not held to the equipment of our culture. Like kundalini yogis forcing the semen flow back upstream and upward, they detach the few implements they use from the instrumental complex of civilization, detaching themselves from these very implements even as they fit themselves into them, forcing the power and the mass back upstream, from clenched fist toward drummed vortex of the solar plexus.

The civilizing of the body

Natural evolution elaborated the neurological and physiological potentials in the human primate that made culture – implements, language, social institutions – possible. But *Homo sapiens* is a domesticated species; his nature is civilized. What has civilization done to the biological nature of this primate? Paleontologist Leroi-Gourhan (*Le geste et la parole, technique et langage*) distinguishes four stages in the technological history of our species that have decisively evolved our biological nature. The first stage is that of the use of tools – cutters, choppers, and grinders. The baboons, as all earthbound mammals, advance into the world snout-first; it is with their teeth that they maneuver their way. The human primate put chipped stones in his front legs to cut, to chop, and to grind. He exteriorized the functions of his teeth and powered them with what now becomes hands. He transforms himself biologically into an upright animal feeling his way with his hands, lifting his eyes to survey the distances. At the same time the sense of his nose and the power of his teeth begin their atrophy. The exteriorized teeth, the chipped stones, still have to be maneuvered with muscle power. The next species-decisive stage will be the harnessing of exterior motor power – that of animals, water, and wind – to drive his implements for him. The primacy of the sense of the vision that surveys will be definitively enhanced – even in his sexuality, now, Freud hypostasized, unseasonal for not primarily excited by menstrual odors but by the visually exposed genitals of the upright ape. At the same time his hide thins into skin and his muscles begin their atrophy. But the wind, water, and draft animals that operate his implements instead of his own hands still require his surveillance. The next species-decisive stage will be the invention of machines – contrivances that start and stop, control, and, more and more, correct their operations. This stage begins with the invention of the mechanical clock. Its new virtue, by comparison with the hour-glass and clepsedra, is that it recycles itself, and can trigger other movements. The first clock-makers of Europe immediately set out to construct clocks which filled towers and, as they struck the hour, opened doors from which the three kings and the four horsemen of the Apocalypse advanced and gesticulated, while the cathedral clarion tolled above without a bell-ringer. Mechanisms now liberate humans from their surveillance – and the attention-span of machine-age humans begins its atrophy. Television-viewers, their fingers on channel-change knobs, today look with incomprehension at Guatamalan Indians whose attention may be held on the patterns of a loom for hours on end. Still, the surveillance mechanisms have to be programmed by the neurological circuitry of the human brain. Today our technological civilization has entered into a cybernetics revolution – which is also a new stage of our biological evolution. Computers henceforth assemble and evaluate the data, and make the decisions. The faculty of memory, reason, and decision, evolved in our nature through the history of our civilization, now begins its atrophy. The film *The Terminator* is set a generation from now, when the master-computers deciding the racing of the military-industrial complex now determine the use of all resources and of the human species. A band of guerrilla resistors, led by John O'Connor, is waging operations of sabotage against the cybernetic police. The master-computers select the Terminator (Arnold Schwarzenegger) to be time-projected back into the twentieth century with a mission to terminate the life of Sarah O'Connor, John O'Connor's mother, and thus ensure that the guerrilla leader will never be born. The human species has, with the next evolution of its technological civilization, undergone regression back into manpower, and the film plots its retrogressive abortion as a biological species endowed with initiative. This film is in fact no science-fiction fantasy; today the stockpiling of weapons of extinction is the most important sector of our industry, and its exponential advance is already programmed by internal feed-back circuitry. This forty-year-old industry has already stockpiled nuclear weapons enough to detonate a Hiroshima-size thermonuclear bomb over a city of our civilization every day for the next three thousand five hundred years. The equivalent of the annual production of the poorest fifth of toiling mankind is now devoted to weapons – the total productive energy of one human being employed to fabricate weapons to exterminate the other four. Certainly not our fellow-citizens, but not their political leaders either, are in control of the military industry; our Secretary of Defense awaits the data electronically satellite-espionaged from the Soviet Union to be processed by the Pentagon computers, and they will make the decisions as to what new weapons our technology must fabricate; the Soviet Presidium similarly only relays the decisions. We have already evolved into pure spectators, the Mouse Folk Kafka imagined, with huge eyes feeding into massive brains, floating in the air, with minuscule, atrophied limbs dangling. Or rather, our sight disconnected from any decision or motor functions, its content determined by the image-industry programming, hoisted into the space of visibility on the massive trunks of cybernetic forests – our bulbous and succulent organisms biologically evolving, Leroi-Gourhan says, into orchids. Organisms with atrophied trunks and limbs, parasitically clinging to the rising trunks that shut out the sun, flowering their huge showy sex organs, awaiting the bees for their orgasmic unions. But is not the glorification of our primary and secondary sexual splendors – the orchid-woman flowering against the hood of the Mercedes, the orchid-man flowering under the sky-diver parachute – also destined to lose their biological relevance and atrophy, in the measure that the flickering computer chips of biological engineering, and not our physiological ostentations, which will decide which genes will be reproduced?

Every great epoch of culture, Nietzsche wrote, is not only an epoch of humankind's cultivating of nature – transforming of nature's resources in accordance with its own idea – it is also an epoch in the history of humankind's cultivation of its own nature – transforming its own nature in accordance with its ideal. Every great culture, marked by distinctive intellectual, artistic and moral productions, has also set up a distinctive icon of bodily perfection. The physical ideal of the yogi, of the lion-maned moran of the African savannah, of the serpent-plumed Mayas, of the olympians of the age of Pericles, of the samurai, of the baris knights of Bali – each great center of culture has set up the corrals, perfected and breeding and training methods, ordered the subjugations and the testings for its own body ideal. In the new institutions specific to modern Western society – barracks, factories, public schools, prisons, hospitals, asylums – Foucault identified the specifically modern ideal of the *disciplined body*.

All these ideal bodies have now become obsolete. Yukio Mishima remarked on the anomaly of the cult of body-building; it appeared in Japan only after the defeat of the Second World War, the last samurai fantasy – that is, in a Japan where massive musculature is without employ in high-tech industry and pointless in a nation whose constitution forbids any remilitarization. It is, indeed, irrelevant across our planet without such constitutions, where the next war will be won or lost (more exactly, reciprocally lost) by fingers pushing buttons, and where in the hour it will last there will be no occasion for ingenius strategic plans, skillful tactics, heroic feats of endurance, or non-participation.

The cause, the adventure, the corrida

There is a pervasive resentment of the exhibitionism of body-builders. It is not a resentment of physical exhibitionism; human nature in our epoch is cultivated especially by means of the glorification of athletes, female nudity, and feats of physical bravado.

A cause wins with the athlete – the school, the French nationalized automative industry, the nation-state, the free-market world. In the team-instincts of football players, the tail-gaters read the name of a brand of beer that is on their own gregarious chests too; in the personal engineering of mountain-climbers the telespectators read the name of a multinational corporation in which they are programmed stockholders; in the single-mindedness of boxers they read the ruling finality of one of those multi-corporation consortiums with a world-market in view called nations. The bodies of athletes are causes. They are also feed-back loops in the marketing industry. Achievement comes from the computer-revealed genetic potential, individually computerized diet and training, drugs and publicity and marketing. The purely abstract, formal, numerical, causes of their competitions feed into the causes of the rising and falling stocks of multinational enterprises.

At Penn State, which I found myself honored to belong to by readers of newspapers in London, Tokyo, Singapore, and

Managua who exulted in its Number One football team, Ken Graves attends a body-building meet at the local high school; he reports that not even the high-school kids were there, only the body-builders, their siblings, and their spouses. The amateurs Ken Graves is interested in have no patrons and train and go to exhibitions at their own expense, which the trophy received by the top one of the class will not reimburse; even the world-class professionals can earn extra dividends as ad lay-out models only for barbell companies and vitamin-supplement products bought by the other body-builders. Ken Graves's camera encounters them pumping and oiling themselves in the delapidated movie theaters of small towns, in locker-rooms covered with graffiti and in classrooms whose blackboards are covered with musical scales and high-school geometry formulas. Indeed the public imagination depicts them as fixated adolescents in high-school locker-rooms after hours. In the absence of a public cause before them and before us, the public mind can only rummage around for psychological causes producing these cases – distorted father-figure, anti-social underworld instincts sublimated by fear of the police, fixated libidinal compulsations. One sees them narcissistically pumping themselves into ostentatious sex symbols – but symbols the sexually liberated public recognizes as the obsolete figure of virile protector, who was also phallocrat and wife-beater. When the mind finds itself seduced to look where there is no cause inscribed, it turns away in resentment.

What is she trying to prove, that woman who has gotten herself hung up on a centimeter here a centimeter there on her calves and neck? The image-industry of our time instead glorifies the exhibitionism of the unathletic – female but not male – body. The nudity of the male athlete is a locker-room nudity before or after the competition, just the time to buy or sell a Marlboro. The nudity of the male non-athlete is that justified baring of the arms to operate machinery, baring of the legs for speed, stripping for underwater welding. The precision-tooling gives the male body seriousness and seemliness; the axis of bravery can give it nobility. Without the gearing-into the tool – or without a vision of bravery at grips with death – unathletic male nudity is ridiculous. But the female anatomy verges on the ridiculous too, as our advertizing, our high art, and our pornography know; it has to be relayed with stage props – be they reduced to the minimum, as in Noh theater, to high-heeled shoes, a garter, atmosphere spread with vaseline on the camera lens, or, as Marilyn Monroe said, perfume. With the props that female anatomy is exhibited in a theater, where acts – be they that of lying there, indolent and fatuous – have consequences and weave a plot. The theater of adventure is a space maintained alongside the politico-economic fields of our enterprises. Maleness is exhibited in an enterprise, where the causes that produce results are also the causes of our industrious and mercantile zones; femaleness is denuded in a theater, where the causes are aleatory and the chain of consequencs an adventure. Secretively, clouded with gauzy sunlight, or brazenly, in front of a castoff nurse's uniform, female nudity is a cause in the plot of an adventure which justifies it. The voyeur, crouched behind his telescope lined up with the windows of the building opposite, or crouched before his videoscreen, thinks not of blue-prints, data, and will-power, but dreams of luck and white magic, believes the chemistry of alchemical legends, the chance encounters by which an ineluctable destiny in the time of horoscopes is deciphered. He fiercely resents those women who, rebuilding their bodies out of muscle, are ruining the anatomy of the central character required for the theater of adventure.

But what about the corrida? No woman spread-eagled in a stripshow is as brazenly exhibited as the matador in the corrida. His body and his blood are exalted in a monstrance of scarlet velvets, spun-silver lace, and jewels over against the black fury of the bull. Insolence flaunts his torso, contempt splays his thighs, flash-fires of foolhardy intelligence crackle across his tensed and cynical posturings. His testicles and penis jeweled in the codpiece and provocatively exposed to the lusts of the crowds. It is, Hemingway says, not gladiatorial spectacle, but tragic theater. It also became this only in our time. Only a century ago did the corrida change from being an activity of aristocrats for the sake of killing bulls into a theater for the extreme glorification of the torero, whose splendor blazes not in the ecstatic love of killing (the love of, and consequently the gift for, killing is, Hemingway reports, all but obsolete in the legendary matadors of our time), but in the sovereign power to lead the raging horns of the doomed bull to his own brandished torso and to a torrent of blood and death at his feet.

Hemingway misleads us where he tells us to think of it not as

Roman gladiatorial spectacle but Greek tragic theater. Greek tragic theater is not a theater for the exhibition of deeds, but for the ineluctable revelation of a concealed truth. The death of the hero is decided by a destiny that the spectators are induced to grasp with a higher intelligence, which the insertion of the individual into a cosmic order or providence or political cause made possible. In the corrida it is not the death of the torero but that of the bull that is plotted, in the third act, within fifteen minutes of the opening of the gates. The facts are that all the toreros do get gored, but most die of syphilis or tuberculosis. The death present in this Black Mass is not a sacrificial death; it is not the Orphic death of a god by which his power will pass into the cosmic order; it is not the intelligible exposition of death in nature where the dying of one organism is its redistribution into others; it is not a cultural death where a dynasty, an age, a revolution triumphs through or perishes with the death of the tragic hero. Here there is not a solitary life that confronts its place in a revolution, a kingdom of God, or the cosmic order; there is an animality in which nothing is visible but a condensation of the ferocity of nature, a single-minded and brave, unretreating rage that drives the bull to his death, but which has made of the organization of life in him the most powerful in nature. The corrida then is not a theater with a plot of interactions to be intelligibly grasped, nor a truth to be deduced from events, nor a confused spectacle to be understood in narrative order, with beginning, middle, and end; it is a ritual of atavist nature, in the time of repetition, the time of In the Beginning. What is true is that it is the inner force that calls forth death that here is revealed as what the male body is made of. This force is the dark blood of nobility that swells the phallic anatomy. All the minor arts of costume and jewelry, or choreographed mannerisms and mani-curing, all the flattering cultivation of patronage and the priming of critics with gifts, which would make an athlete fall to the ridiculous, do not tarnish but set off the dark light of nobility in his exposed carnality. The ritual of the torero is made of precise and complex and instantaneously discharged intelligence, to be sure, and neurological precision, and the impeccable taste breeding and not training can produce, and the unwavering force of valor. All this is visibly inscribed on, is sustained by, or produces an epiphany of arrogant and fateful phallic sexuality. It is virility erected in splendor at the brink of raging death.

What our culture's mind can understand is a *virile body*, a body where virility is virtù, the primary virtue of courage. Socrates at his trial, where the virtue or aberrancy of his pedagogical enterprise was to be defended, instead spoke of his courage in battle, which all his fellow-citizens knew. Aristotle was to explain further, when in the *Nicomachean Ethics* he put courage first in the list of virtues, that courage is the transcendental virtue, the condition for the possibility of all the others; without courage neither honesty nor magnanimity nor service nor even wit in conversation are possible. But all courage, the courage to endure physical pain as the courage required to make decisions, is but the ramification of the courage in the face of death. It is through the power to hold one's own posture as the ground gives way beneath one that every power to take a stand is derived. Is it not the dim sense that all the causes and works of civilization are so many ideals or idols set up to defy death, that the virtues of laborers and of athletes, inasmuch as they are ways of holding firm when pain assaults and when the support of the others gives way, are derivative of the power to withstand the confrontation with death, that saves us from seeing under the glory we flood on their bodies a ridiculous anatomy? Is not the corrida a ritual in which this dim intuition is maintained in the midst of our laborious culture which only produces comfort and security?

There is then perhaps in our resentment of them a dim sense that the cult of the body-builders desecrates the ritual structure with which we maintain dignity in and disperse ridicule from our physical nature. The public does not see in body-builders ferocious and destructive brutes which offend its sacralization of civilization – they are known to use their massive power as guardians of bourgeois property, taking jobs, typically, as night watchmen and bouncers in nightclubs where the rich idle; and they are suspected of being steroid-pumped eunuchs from whom the debutants have nothing to fear. But the resentment senses in them a virility insulated from death. Years of training that led to no corrida, only to the footlights of a high-school stage. Rather than a brave contest with death, a sentimental fantasy of immortality on glossy photographs, fetishized into the metal figures of trophies. The duelling scars obligatory in German university students of the last century confirmed the nobility of their caste; the steel of the body-builder's equipment is nothing but inertia, exorcised of the death that forged the saber. There is a feeling at large that the musculature gained in work and in rule-governed contests, the bodies of construction workers, deep-sea divers, and boxers, is virile and virtuous; the musculature built in the rituals of the body-builder's cult grotesque.

The hands of the body-builders do not contend with the inertia of implements or weapons, but rise to unfold in the sunlight or fold to frame their great swollen bosoms; beneath their wasp-waists their legs pirouette; Arnold Schwarzenegger studied in a ballet studio how to walk with the grace of a prima donna. The discomfort voiced today before the new breed of women body-builders betrays the vision of the hermaphrodite that one meant when one called the excessive anatomy of the male body-builders 'grotesque'. Psychoanalyst Julia Kristeva, after viewing the film *Commando*, spoke of how explicit this has now become, Arnold Schwarzenegger in happy domesticity, tender, caring, feeding his child – no mention of a woman that would have given birth to this child or of what had become of her. The body-builder not only stands in phallic hardness; he or she also moves rhythmically with the tensed violence of labor pains.

Is it not true that this body is not ennobled with the contention of power with death within it, toward birth? Bringing the dead weight of the steel within his/her muscles, the body-builder brings him/herself ever closer to that limit determined by birth. One's genes harbor another death, an inner death; as soon as we are born we are old enough to die, says an ancient wisdom. In pushing back to the genetic coding of the genus, one pushes one's way to the death sentence written in the individual by the immortality of the genetic formula. The living organism, Freud taught, discharges its forces to ward off the death exterior to it only in order to seek its own death, its own advance to the death that is its own. The courage that forces one into this internal death, this death that is one's own, is the very courage with which one is born. Freud was only thinking that every living organism has a lifespan that is indistinguishable from its definition as a species, even though its life-forces are so many resistances to the death-dealing blows that fall upon it from without; the sequoias are not killed by the lightning that strikes them every year and burns out their cores; the seed was programmed to live for two thousand years, and then to die. But the body-builder tears down, muscle-system by muscle-system, all the strength in his/her fibers and cells against the death of the steel, and he/she knows that the hard will that takes him/her all the way to the limits of his/her exhaustion is the very movement by which power, and new, greater, power is born. His/her work, his/her feats, are nothing but labor pains; and he/she knows what is genetically coded to be born in him/her only in knowing the time and the effort it takes to leave all his/her force on the dead inertia of the steel. There is then in the force with which the body-builder assumes all that is and could have been born in him/her also a courage and a splendor. Even if, viewed from the outside, it appears as the monstrous excrescence of maternity in the virile figure of power.

The surfacing of splendor

Monstrous – that is, not only the anomalous and the gigantic, but the ostentatious (monster, *monstrare*). This anomalous, gigantic, and ostentatious figure would be the way the cult overcomes derision before the evolution of the human anatomy reduced to nature. Is not the conviction that our anatomy, ridiculous by nature, has to serve as the material for art coextensive with all civilization?

The civilization our species has launched to relay its evolution appears in nature not only as the exteriorization of the powers in our organs but also as the exteriorization of the splendors in the periodicity of our impulses. Leroi-Gourhan divines that the first art is the most inward – an artistry done on one's visceral core in the yoga of Mohenjodaro and Harappa four thousand years ago, an artistry that condensed chant or invocation into a mantra which is sounded only inwardly, which concentrated the periodic motility of the body into the scanned rhythms of the circulation of air and blood and semen. The compulsion for ordering the circulation of men and goods in outer, public space, which Freud found contemporary with the first beginnings of civilization, and which he attributed to the compulsion of the principle of economy, we would rather see to be an exteriorization of the sense of inner rhythm and circulation which were the materials for the first artistry our species worked on its own nature. The first artists worked, Nietzsche said, with the noblest clay and oil, the artist's own flesh and blood.

The epochs of the splendors of civilization appear to Leroi-Gourhan to be epochs of the progressive exteriorization of this inwardly-working artistic compulsion. Thus the art of body movement and vocalization, dance and song, would issue from the older visceral artistry of the yogis. Glorification of the body-surfaces exposed to view comes out of the distant epochs where dance and song were the media for our species' self-glorification; making of the body-surfaces a collage of bird-of-paradise plumes and boars' tusks, or a cuneiform tablet of tattooings and scarifications is an artistry that arises in a culture of festivity and chant. A next stage of exteriorization is that of the architectonic splendors of Babylonian, Athenian, Mayan, Ottoman, and Gothic culture, which honored as major artists those who frame the construction and urban lay-out that houses human movements. The art exteriorized on surface effects – in the age when those who are preeminently called artists are painters – the 'humanist' art of the European Renaissance and subsequent modern period of painting, was in fact an artistry worked on the exterior spectacle as blocked off and framed into a perspective by the human eye. Now the buildings man's earlier artistry had surrounded him with serve as the points of departure for an artistic eye that orders into splendor the views from the balconies and the towers. Our contemporary art now extends itself beyond the perspective spread out before the human sense organs to the spaces reached for by the mind and by its electronic relays – to microcosmic and macrocosmic exteriority. Contemporary art is conceptual, framing the designs of microchemistry and astronomy; contemporary music captures the songs of the whales and those of the earth's magnetic field.

The meaning and the origin of the drive productive of splendor seemed to Freud as enigmatic as it seemed certainly coextensive with the defensive and utilitarian drives that transform nature and transform our nature. Living things are not only equipped with organs to perceive what is exterior; they are also equipped with organs designed to be perceived. Splendor, if created by the chance coincidence of random events in a canyon in a desert, in a sunset over equatorial waters, is also an organic production of living things. This was the thesis of Adolph Portman, who argued that the patterns of animal body-surfaces have their own intelligibility. The morphology of the inner, functional body, the form and the arrangement of the skeleton, of the respiratory, circulatory, digestive, and reproductive organs, and of the prehensile and locomotive organs, does not make intelligible the always regular and often intricate and ostentatious patterns of the body-surfaces and extremities. These have to be understood, he argues, as organs-to-be-seen, whose designs and colors become intelligible only when we correlate them with the specific powers and the witness-organs for which they are contrived. The inwardly coiling horns of the mountain sheep and the hairless, protuberant buttocks of the baboons are, he says, organs as closely fitted to the eyes and lips of the spectator as the jaws and hoofs are fitted to the terrain and the specific foods of the species.

In the human primate, a distinctive reflexive circuit was set up with the evolution of the hand. The human species began by putting the cutter, chopper and grinder functions of the jaws into its hands. The front legs no longer serve to drive the jaws to make contact with the world; they rise from the ground and conduct samplings of the world to the head. The human animal now acquires a face. Its muscular configurations no longer react immediately to the front-line of contact with external nature, but turns to its own hands. A smile and an apprehensive grimace now become possible – movements that are *expressive*, that is, that address a sample, a representative of the independent exterior held in the hand – and, soon, held with a mental grasp before an inner eye. An animal that faces considers representations it has apprehended. Its manual musculature becomes not only prehensile but also expressive; the hands position their take for an appraising eye. They address themselves also to the eyes of another animal that has acquired a face; they speak. Little by little our whole musculature has learned to speak. The throat muscles designed for devouring and for expelling substances and the body's own biles and rages now learns from the hands how to shape the samples and representatives of the outside, how to exteriorize the comprehensive expressions the hands first learned to make. The whole torso becomes organs-to-be-seen, the abdomen struts and cowers, the legs and thighs acquire humility and pride, the shoulders and back, turned from the face-to-face circuit, sway with resentment and defiance.

Unlike the birds-of-paradise and the mountain sheep and the baboons, the human species did not develop distinctive organs-to-be-apprehended in addition to its organs-for-apprehending. Its hair, become functionally obsolete, is in an advanced state of disappearance; it has not deviated into a patterned pelt. Its teeth, whose functions were exteriorized onto tools, are in an advanced state of atrophy, and have not deviated into coiling tusks to make impressive the face. With the upright posture, Freud assumed, the primate genitals are permanently exhibited to the frontal view of another, and, Freud assumed, this has led to the primacy of the eyes over the smell as the chief organ for sexual stimulation, and the end of a rutting season, the unseasonableness of human libido. Yet the human genitals remain organs fitted for contact, and have not become expressive organs. To be sure, the human species has contrived snares for the eye – penis sheaths, cache-sexes, pendants hung over the breasts – but these are exterior to its own genitalia, which remain glandular, orifices of the inner, functional body.

What has happened is that it is the human muscular system that has taken on the second, expressive, role for which the other animals have evolved distinctive organs-to-be-seen. The human muscular system is not only the scaffolding that positions and turns the sense organs, the organs-for-apprehending; the vectors and surges of motor energy illuminate the muscular network itself and make its mesh and mounds snares for the eye. On human bodies muscle frettings are their peacock tails, curls worked on the lips their crests, biceps and pectorals their coiled horns, finger-waverings their lustrous pelt.

But civilization, in that epoch when the hunter-gatherers mutated into self-domesticated animals, altered the human muscular system. As it exteriorized motor efficacy from the human muscles to the animal, wind, water, and steam-power that relayed them, it exteriorized the ostensive functioning of muscles into masks, talismans, and costume.

To be sure, this exteriorization has not yet become complete and definitive; there still floats in civilization an imagination that feeds on muscles. Indeed the imagination, that unpenetrating, superficial vision, vision of surfaces without depth, is a *faculty of the muscles*. Mishima spoke of the *displacement* of his sense of himself when, an intellectual, he committed himself to body-building; there is a specific sense of one's identity that rises out of the visceral or cerebral depths to find itself henceforth in the contours one's substance spreads out to the sun. This self, spread in the tensions of the musculature, doubles them up as imagination, inhabiting the fascinated with forms, patterns, surfaces, a fascination anchored in the image one oneself forms. And muscles are not exposed without doubling up their surfaces before the imagination of another. It is the first effect of their reality; their contours excite the imagination before they displace resistances. That the visceral system does not have such an effect can seem puzzling. The awareness of the content of fluids in us, of the saline and mineral composition of ocean water, the inner gulf streams, currents, and tides, the coral reefs, channels lined with tentacled anemones, and floating plankton within does not double up our sense of ourselves with a vision of the oceans from which tide pools now enclosed in a porous sack of skin – our muscles have carried us. In fact the imagination is not divinatory and does not penetrate the deep; it is a surface-sense, its mirages mirroring superficial mappings of the terrain, excited by the contours of muscles. And our muscles, becoming more and more obsolete in mechanized industry and automated war, become the more designed for the faculty of imagination.

With the obsolescence of an epic imagination does there not flourish now only a tropical erotic imagination? The Marlboro man, a torso hardened, according to the legend, by riding the range, is perhaps a torso riding the range in order to be hardened into a Marlboro model. The editorial writers of *Playboy* and *Playgirl* declare that the anatomies they exhibit have been fashioned by Olympic nautical training and ocean sailing; but swimming, sailing, bicycling (on stationary machines before mirrors), and work-outs on universal gyms are perhaps designed to produce play musculature. Is the human muscle sheath, strapped to machines, monitored by cardiovascular and fat-ratio dials, turning into the showy carnal corollas and petals of human orchids?

This evolutionary destiny is unclear; the future is complicated by the existence of the cults. In them the body-substance is turned into muscle everywhere, the glands of the abdomen and its coiled membranes into muscles that can parry the blows of a fist, the atrophied mammary glands of males into matrices of trust and power, the chords of the neck are not neglected, nor the threads pulling the fingers. But the body-builders use the most elementary bars and weights; to this day no world-class body-builder has trained on the Nautilus machinery scientific intelligence has designed for them. These are atavist bodies, halted before the age of the self-domestication of the hunter-gatherer. We found no real difference between the scene in Gold's Gym and on the banks of the Ganges, to which the origins of every method to divinize the mind with every possible cosmological system but also every method to divinize the body with sublunary power can be traced back, where we saw, in 1980, young men making the prostrations before the idols of the Aryan ape-god Hanuman which we term push-ups and calesthenics, and, while intoning mantras, lifting before him rocks and pairs of millstones fixed on poles. Cults where we see not body-mechanisms made on machines, but primogenitor bodies made of *the elemental* – the weight of the terrestrial, and rivers, and sun.

The body-builder's implements do not relay the passage of his/her own body-force outward. He/she confronts the steel, the opaque, inert mineralization of death, with all his/her animate power, in what is no contest but a process of symbiosis or synthanatosis. He/she tears down his/her muscles on steel, exhausting all his/her force on it, and when muscle failure has been reached, receives from the metal its properties. His/her biceps become tempered flails, his pectorals, that is, his mammaries, his femaleness, become gearing, the membrane of his/her abdomen a sheet of corrugated steel, his/her knuckles themselves brass. The luster of his/her muscle-contours acquire for the eye the opaque impenetrability of metal. At the same time in the repetitions, the contractions and flexions, the body-builder internalizes into channels of surging power the fluidity of the sweat and the oils, the vaporous currents of steam, showers, surf, and sunlight. The power that holds him/her upright is no longer that of a post before the equipment that civilization has erected. Tide-pools of the maternal ocean enclosed in a porous sack of skin carried up to dry land by developing muscles, they stand erect now with the form that a fountain maintains by the incessant upsurge and fall of streams of power.

The body-builder senses his/her identity on the bronzed, electrolytic luster of the beams of musculature exposed to the sun; it is on the sweat-sheets across this hard skin and the surface-gleam of the sun, and on the surfaces of mirrors displaying the oiled definition that he/she now seeks him/herself. Existence, for the self, no longer means inwardness, visceral or cerebral involution, but exposure. This self is a movement to extend itself across contours and forms, and not to maintain a point of view, a repair in space. As the ego surfaces, distends and exposes itself, it depersonalizes. Not only does the steel transfer its own properties to the living tissue that has exhausted its own force on it; its homogeneity also drives out the principles of individuality in the bodies that devote themselves to it. It does away with the eccentricities – the dry and irritable skin, the concave faint-hearted chest, the indolent stomach, the furtive hand, the shifting eye – by which movements of retreat set up the as-for-me of individuality and leave their marks on the body. On his/her contours the body-builder watches emerging not the eccentricities his tastes and vices leave in his carnal substance, but the lines of force of the generic *human animal*.

How little the rest of us see of our bodies! Our genitals we conceal, even from ourselves, judging them, with Leonardo da Vinci, of an irremediable ugliness; our visceral and glandular depths, the inner coral reefs and pulsating channels of antennas and gyrating polyps, our very imagination blinds itself to. Our musculature we attend to with a clinician's or mechanic's inspection. The drive to visibility, to highnoon exposure, is so alien to us that it has to be driven into our substance by the steel. Ken Graves speaks of the watch-maker eye body-builders have for the individual components. They do not, like the rest of us, see charm or brutality; their eye is specialized for details, trained in instant measurings, intolerant of dissymmetries. As they wait in the wings for the decisions of the judges, the contestants line up, he says, in almost exactly the order the judges will have placed them. As though it is not the individual eye permanently fixed in a point of view and a perspective that sees, but the impersonal eye of a species in evolution appraising its organs and limbs for an advance whose duration and direction are unknown. Body-builders look at one another, and each at himself/herself, also with an alchemist's eye full of chemical formulas, protein supplement-ations, quack remedies inspired by analogies, and drugs made in biochemical laboratories. They know their muscle substance with a cellular and not general and conceptually formulated knowledge, with a knowledge that thinks in the pain of cells being stretched and elongated, being torn down, a knowledge that does not preside over yet somehow accompanies the invisible movements of the millions of anti-bodies within which are the real cause and reality of the separateness of our bodies.

One does not know what role evolution will find for these prodigies of musculature – or, rather, what evolution their artistry is contriving for the species. No one, Nietzsche wrote, is more readily corrupted than artists. Their souls, their taste, can be bought by venal priests of pagan religions, by the big investors in the image-industry, by the master-computers of the racing military-industrial complex, and by their own followers and flatterers. Today the names of the body-builders whose names are known are the names of so many industries, auxiliary epicycles in the wheels of the planetary machinery.

But the imagination that feeds on muscles imagines something else – imagines that the deviation their cult makes from the path of civilization might be carried further. Civilization destined the self-driving power of human bodies to be transferred into tools, and then to be transferred out of human muscles into draft animals, wind, water, steam, atomic fission. At this late date, the body-builders reverse the movement, disconnect from the tools, having interiorized their elemental properties, and make of musculature a splendor. Civilization destined the powers of surveillance in human sense organs to be directed on the motor force now exteriorized in draft animals, windmills and water-wheels, electric and atomic-fission generators, and then to be transferred out of human sense organs into automatic and feed-back mechanisms. Can we imagine at some future date the eyes, the touch, the heart disconnecting from the machinery that feeds in the images and the information, and swell and glow with their own resplendence? Civilization evolved the faculty of memory, reason, and decision, and destined it to program the electronic sensors and feed-back mechanisms that make the human sense organs obsolete. Can we imagine at some future date the faculty of memory, reason, and decision disconnecting from the computers which it now serves, ceasing to be but an organ-for-apprehending, and, swollen with its own wonders, become an organ-to-be-apprehended, orchid rising from the visceral and cerebral depths of the cybernetic forest with its own power, rising into the sun?

· 7 ·

'Ideal Selfishness'
Nietzsche's Metaphor
of Maternity

ALISON AINLEY

Throughout Nietzsche's texts the metaphors of pregnancy proliferate, images of 'forming, maturing, perfecting', a 'secret task'[1]
most commonly aligned with what Nietzsche terms the 'ideal
selfishness' of creativity, and hence with the Greek image of the
artist or philosopher 'giving birth' to an idea or a work. In Plato's
Symposium, Diotima borrows the metaphor of pregnancy to
furnish the notion of creativity as immortality, the eternal
perpetuation of life as the child, the work.[2] Pregnancy is a symbol
of eternity. However, given Nietzsche's suspicion of the transcendental ideal inherent in such a notion, it is clear that Nietzsche
could not take up the metaphor unproblematically, despite his
nostalgia and admiration for the 'Ancients'.[3] Nietzsche is scornful
of the notion of creativity as passive, subordinated production,
because it implies a will to 'go beyond', a move towards
immortality which could-be construed as a denial of the body and
the pain at hand. And yet Nietzsche seems to affirm the
preoccupation of the potentially creative being with its own care
and responsibility as a positive state or mode of behaviour.

Thus on the one hand the metaphors of pregnancy inform
Nietzsche's attitudes towards creativity. Yet on the other hand
they also have bearing on the metaphors of women. At certain
points Nietzsche appears to reduce women to their reproductive
capacity alone – Zarathustra advises the old woman: 'Everything

about woman is a riddle and everything about woman has one
solution: it is called pregnancy.'[4] In other places he suggests that
the relation of mother to child provides the potentiality of a re-
thought ethical relation to others. It is this aspect of the metaphor
I wish to consider, in the light of Derrida's reading of sexual
difference and metaphor in Nietzsche's texts, and feminist
considerations of the symbolism of maternity. To this end, I
reproduce in full a section from *Daybreak* which introduces the
metaphor's problematic status:

Ideal selfishness – Is there a more holy condition than that of
pregnancy? To do all we do in the unspoken belief that it has somehow to
benefit that which is coming to be within us! – has to *enhance* its
mysterious worth, the thought of which fills us with delight! In this
condition we avoid many things without having to force ourselves very
hard! We suppress our anger, we offer the hand of conciliation, our child
shall grow out of all that is gentlest and best. We are horrified if we are
sharp or abrupt; suppose it should pour a drop of evil into the dear
unknown's cup of life! Everything is veiled, ominous, we know nothing of
what is taking place, we wait and try to be *ready*. At the same time, a
pure and purifying feeling of profound irresponsibility reigns in us almost
like that of the auditor before the curtain has gone up – *it* is growing, *it* is
coming to light, *we* have no right to determine either its value or the hour
of its coming. All the influence we can exert lies in keeping it safe. 'What
is growing here is something greater than we are' is our most secret hope:
we prepare everything for it so that it may come happily into the world:
not only everything that may prove useful to it, but also the joyfulness
and laurel wreaths of our soul. It is in this *state of consecration* that one
should live! It is a state one can live in! And if what is expected is an idea,
a deed – towards every bringing forth we have essentially no other
relationship than that of pregnancy and ought to throw to the winds all
presumptuous talk of 'willing' and 'creating'. This is *ideal selfishness*;
continually to watch over and care for and to keep our soul still, so that
our fruitfulness shall *come to a happy fulfilment*! Thus, as intermediaries,
we watch over and care for to *the benefit of all*: and the mood in which
we live, this mood of pride and gentleness, is a balm which spreads far
around us and into our restless souls too. But the pregnant are *strange*! So
let us be strange too, and let us not hold it against others if they have to
be so! And even if the outcome is dangerous and evil, let us not be less
reverential towards that which is coming to be than worldly justice is,
which does not permit a judge or an executioner to lay hands on one who
is pregnant![5]

Is there anything to be salvaged here other than re-marking the means of paying off women who might struggle to express dissatisfaction with motherhood as it is understood and reproduced – the means of advising the powerless of their superior ethical status? Dismissing the section in this way would be in line with a general dismissal of Nietzsche's comments on women. But reading the passage simultaneously as an *affirmation* of women makes it more difficult to assess and leads to an ambiguity in interpretation. This is significant for feminism in that it raises questions not only about the status of women in Nietzsche's writings, but also about the status of interpretation itself.

Commenting on the derogatory nature of the word *Frauenzimmer* which appears in a section in *The Gay Science*, Walter Kaufmann writes: 'This whole sentence, like many of Nietzsche's generalisations about women, descends to a lower level – stylistically as well as in content. It seems to be intended merely to lead up to the pun that follows it.'[6] Kaufmann's apology to women may now seem not only shamefaced but misplaced, in the sense that it reduces the complexity and caution advocated elsewhere in reading Nietzsche to a simple equation of representation, a correspondence of 'word' to 'thing'. Such a reading might well engender indignation and anger, placing Nietzsche within a philosophical tradition of misogyny.[7] But the directness of such an approach refuses to consider that Nietzsche's account of, and position in, such a movement is extremely problematic. Nietzsche's constant implication of language in the metaphysical systems he explores and exposes cannot be put aside for 'the question of woman'. On one level a feminist reader of Nietzsche might recognise those women who permeate and perforate the Nietzschean texts as 'herself'; *my* self. On another level a feminist critique which wishes to question the singular, unified self implicated with patriarchal systems cannot accept a purely mimetic view of language and consequently requires a more complex understanding of 'woman' in Nietzsche's writings.

In Derrida's book *Spurs/Éperons* the enactment of these modes of criticism results in a third mode, characterised by the active affirmation of the changing, shifting, metaphoric, creative phenomena of 'woman'.

In the instance of the third proposition, however, beyond the double negation of the first two, woman is recognised as an affirmative power, a dissimulatress, an artist, a dionysiac. And no longer is it man who affirms her. She affirms herself, in and of herself, in man.[8]

The double edge of the affirmation of women/creativity as *life*, the *vita femina* is on the one hand a positive celebration of the birth of culture from the inward care of that which is 'coming to be'; on the other hand, the 'veiled, ominous' aspect which, together with 'profound irresponsibility', corresponds to Nietzsche's notion of 'truth-as-woman',[9] the equivocal and allusive figure to whom only those who seek with the dogged determination of the philosopher would be tempted to ascribe an essence. Nietzsche's affirmation of the Dionysian, dizzying, dithyrambic rhythms of life involves his becoming a mother, a woman, and yet, in the mode of Dionysus, a god assuming the veils of disguise through metaphor. 'Dionysus adopts Apollo's veil and his enigmatic visage; a necessary shift from one divinity to another that could, strictly, be called metaphor, especially since Nietzsche expresses this in a language that is above all Apollonian – the metaphorical discourse, poetic and imagist'.[10]

Derrida offers a timely meditation on the metaphorical status of women in Nietzsche's writings. He suggests that Nietzsche makes an ironic equation of women with the transcendental absolutes he is concerned to explore and expose. But this is tied to 'the question of style' – a strategic appropriation of qualities historically and culturally associated with women (feminity) in writing. Derrida takes up the equivalence of woman and truth, the truth of woman, which is not a closure of equivalence because neither is taken to have a complete and distinct identity. Instead, there is shifting ambiguity and plurality – no one woman, no one truth, no one style. The congealment of truth into fixity or essence is countered by the notion of 'a mobile army of metaphors, metonyms and anthropomorphisms'.[11] And because such a plurality might be construed as a simple negation of principled singularity, Derrida suggests that Nietzsche parodies even his own 'truths'.[12] For the reversal, if it is not accompanied by a discrete parody, a strategy of writing, or diffrence, or deviation in quills, if there is no style, no grand style, this is finally but the same thing, nothing more than a clamorous declaration of the antithesis. Hence the heterogeneity of the text.'[13]

The possibility of opening perceptions of the 'feminine', 'coded as that which exceeds the grasp of the Cartesian subject'[14] to use the critical edge apparently accompanying such an excess, is part of the force of the feminine metaphor as it is deployed in Nietzsche's and Derrida's texts. The metaphor is already contained in the horizon of a philosophy of difference, part of a system of oppositions, whereby it is already allusively other. This can be seen in Nietzsche's ironic exposure of the metaphor's historical process, a progressive forgetting of its genealogy. In the section in *Twilight of the Idols* entitled 'How the "True World" Finally became Fable, The History of an Error', he writes: '(Progress of the idea: it grows more refined, more enticing, more incomprehensible – *it becomes woman*, it becomes Christian)'[15] The emphatic phrase '*sie wird Weib*' suggests how it is that the equivalence is made possible. The point at which the idea becomes an entity separable and separated from the 'true world' is the point at which it becomes comparable to an essence of 'woman'. In an opposition between 'the wise, pious, virtuous man' and 'the idea', the essential nature of woman can be identified with that which is other-worldly. The equivalence of this essential figure of woman, the eternal-womanly, with regard to an absolute transcendental value, is further heightened by the feminine gender of the idea and its various manifestations, a parade of veiled allegorical muses:

die Wahrheit	(f)	Truth
die Schönheit	(f)	Beauty
die Ewigkeit	(f)	Eternity
die Weisheit	(f)	Wisdom
die Glückseligkeit	(f)	Happiness
die Idee	(f)	the Idea

If Nietzsche wishes to expose the metaphysical hypostatisation of 'the idea' he is already implicated in writing of 'woman' (she). But this entanglement facilitates the exposure of the hypostatisation of 'Woman', *das Ewig-Weibliche*, which is so far beyond mortality, so far beyond women in the plural and in the world, as to become neuter-neutral. The moment the idea becomes female is the moment that *she* becomes *it*. Nietzsche writes: 'Man created woman – but out of what? Out of a rib of his God, of his "ideal".'[16] And in *The Gay Science*:

> The sage shook his head and smiled. 'It is men', said he, 'that corrupt women; and all the failings of women should be atoned for and improved upon the men. For it is man who creates for himself the image of woman, and woman forms herself according to this image.'[17]

And yet the affirmative mode of 'woman' apparently reinforces the exposure of the Eternal-Womanly in Nietzsche's writing. Having aligned the elusive 'otherness' of woman with the elusive, changeable and alluring transcendent value of truth, Nietzsche affirms and celebrates the continual surface, or that which shifts and changes, through the continual displacement of his own writing. If multiplicity and duplicity are taken to be the 'nature' of woman, then Nietzsche's own strategy can be seen to employ such dissemblance, or what Derrida terms '"l'opération" feminine' (the feminine 'operation').[18] Is it not this displaced and displacing woman, 'figured' in Nietzschean and deconstructive strategies, who simulates orgasm, who defers, differs, demurs even at the truth of this – truth?

Nietzsche writes:

> Reflect on the whole history of women: do they not have to be first of all and above all else actresses? Listen to physicians who have hypnotised women; finally love them – let yourself be 'hypnotised' by them! What is always the end result? That they 'give themselves' even when they – give themselves.[19]
> Woman is so artistic.

And in *Beyond Good and Evil*: 'truth has so much to stifle her yawns here when answers are demanded of her. She is, after all, a woman: one ought not to violate her.'[20]

Derrida plays upon the metaphor of the unviolated hymen for the strategic mis-placing of the centre. If the fulfilment of pleasure, orgasm, is seen as a moment of apparent self-forgetting, but a moment which is also self-confirming, *simulating* this moment can be seen as a series of masks or 'mock' realisations. The possibility of parodying such a process through writing results in a double distancing. In this way the fetish is not dismantled but becomes part of an ironic process of fetishisation.

As Betsey Draine points out in her essay 'Writing, Deconstruction and Other Unnatural Acts',[21] the deferred parodying and masks here imply a move away from sexuality as a 'means towards an end',[22] as conception and reproduction. The privileged line of descent through the child is displaced for the sake of more marginalised activities – a necessary move to deviate from the continuance that is implied in the name of the father. Such strategies do not seek to reproduce themselves as inherited lines of criticism. Derrida takes up Nietzsche's play on the continual surface to play himself at what Draine terms 'sexual deviancy'. Nietzsche indicates his affirmation of such play: 'the philosopher, as the lover, must learn to "stop courageously at the surface, the fold, the skin, to adore appearance, to believe in forms, tones, words, in the whole Olympus of appearance.'[23]

Thus it seems the metaphor of pregnancy should be treated with caution, not only because of the danger of reinstating the patriarchal line of descent, but also because it apparently fills the centre, finds its mark. Pregnancy would be the evidence of penetration – the seed implanted, the surface of the hymen broken, the crude show of the woman who has given herself away'. And yet, to equate the metaphor with passivity, a container awaiting insemination, omits the *active* aspect, the continual and continued potential for creativity and fertility. In his reflections upon the Dionysian, Nietzsche writes:

> *What* did the Hellene guarantee to himself with these mysteries? *Eternal* life, the eternal recurrence of life; the future promised and consecrated in the past; the triumphant Yes to life beyond death and change; true life as collective continuation of life through procreation, through the mysteries of sexuality. It was for this reason that the *sexual* symbol was to the Greeks the symbol venerable as such, the intrinsic profound meaning of all antique piety. Every individual detail in the act of procreation, pregnancy, birth, awoke the most exhalted and solemn feelings. In the teachings of the mysteries, *pain* is sanctified, the 'pains' of childbirth sanctify pain in general all becoming and growing, all that guarantees the future, postulates pain. . . . For the eternal joy in creating to exist, for the will to life to eternally affirm itself, 'the torment of childbirth' *must* also exist eternally.[24]

It is the pain of activity Nietzsche affirms, the contrast to the notion of the philosopher as midwife, passively assisting in the birth of an idea. Despite her superior knowledge, the midwife cannot take over the birth but must give a woman space for her own delivery, and her passive assistance is comparable to the hypostatisation of pregnancy – a reference to the dangers of idealising the Eternal-Womanly as the eternal mother.

> Pregnancy has made women kinder, more patient, more timid, more pleased to submit; and just so does spiritual pregnancy produce the character of the contemplative type, which is closely related to the feminine character; it consists of male mothers.[25]

Nietzsche's re-appropriation of the metaphor takes on the responsibility for pregnancy in himself, to be actively creative, rather than a medium through which ideas are born.' There are among peoples of genius those upon whom has fallen the woman's problem of pregnancy and the secret task of forming, maturing, perfecting – the Greeks, for example, were a people of this kind',[26] and in *Thus Spoke Zarathustra*: 'For one loves from the very heart only one's child, and one's work; and where there is great love of oneself, then it is a sign of pregnancy, thus have I found.'[27]

One aspect of Nietzsche's exposure of 'the old aesthetic' is its passivity, philosophy which is 'content merely to gossip about art'. In this sense the philosopher has 'feminine' traits, or, as Derrida writes: 'he is a sterile woman and certainly not the *männliche Mutter*. Before art, the dogmatic philosopher, a maladroit courtesan, remains, just as did the second-rate scholar, impotent, a sort of old maid.'[28] But, as Derrida adds:

> Nietzsche here is dealing with a very old philosopheme of *production*. And in so doing he is also manipulating its vaguely unnoticed, yet cleverly imitated nuances of creativity, activity, formulation, presentation – its connotations of the formulation and presentation of manifest presence. This concept . . . he inscribes in the analogous equivalence . . . between active, informative productivity and virility on the one hand and material unproductive passivity and femininity on the other. It remains to be seen whether Nietzsche, as it would appear, is indeed contradicting certain of his propositions concerning the woman.[29]

Consequently, it would seem there is an ambiguity in the 'ideal selfishness' which might be read as a confirmation of 'manifest presence', as Derrida writes. But it may also be read as part of the becoming which is 'How to Become What One Is', and as such, part of Zarathustra's teachings of pregnancy and continuous self-overcoming.

You creators, you Higher Men! One is pregnant only with one's own child. . . . The prudence and providence of pregnancy is in your selfishness! What no one has yet seen, the fruit: that is protected and indulged and nourished by your whole love. Where your whole love is, with your child, there too is your whole virtue.[30]

In the final part of the book Zarathustra affirms his own potential pregnancy, and the trace of his children's presence. However, his children are not to be found as followers or disciples who are reproductions of himself, but rather as his own strength of creativity and self-overcoming.

In a number of places Nietzsche indicates the importance of the final section of the third part of *Thus Spoke Zarathustra*, entitled 'The Seven Seals'. It is in this section that 'the greatest weight' of eternal recurrence is conceived, and conceived as Nietzsche's child.

Oh how should I not lust for eternity and for the wedding ring of rings – the Ring of Recurrence! Never did I find the woman by whom I wanted to have children, unless it be this woman, whom I love: For I love you. O Eternity!

For I love you, O Eternity![31]

In his essay 'Traces of Derrida: Nietzsche's Image of Woman',[32] Gayle L. Ormiston equates this passage with Nietzsche's parody or mock-affirmation of the Eternal-Womanly. Perhaps another dimension can be added by considering the ambivalence of the phrase 'by (or from whom) I wanted to have children'. It can be both 'the woman whom I want to have my child', or 'the woman I want to *give me* a child'. If eternal recurrence is Nietzsche's pregnancy it is equivalent to an active affirmation of his self-overcoming. In considering pregnancy as 'ideal selfishness' it seems that Nietzsche invokes a notion of subjectivity as self-absorbed; hence whole to itself, fully represented and self-contained. But the reflection of the pregnant subject upon (her)self is not wholly upon *a* self but upon that which is already other and already strange. It suggests splitting or punctuation, a spacing of a present self where the boundaries of inner and outer become less distinct. Hence the singular, full presence which is the lynchpin and promulgator of phallophilosophy is potentially put into question by the symbolism of pregnancy. The suppression of that which is different and diverse in pregnancy – the laughing, desiring, orgasmic mother – has ensured the continuity of the patrilinear descent, the father's name, through successive generations, which is a relation of sameness. In drawing attention not merely to the repetition of life through pregnancy as stasis, unchanging *passivity*, but as changeable potentiality, Nietzsche suggests a different understanding of its symbolism, an understanding presently contextualised in contemporary French feminism.[33] This re-reading of the metaphor's symbolism marks an alternative to feminist considerations of maternity as the site or even the basis of oppression.[34] While it counters the reduction of women to 'natural mothers', the characteristic of maternity as a barrier to 'real achievement' may also lead to a denial of the body and hence an identification with the forces of repression making pregnancy the subject of what Julia Kristeva terms 'idealised contempt'.[35] She suggests it is important for feminism to claim and explore maternity from, on the one hand, scientific discourse and its objectifying treatment of the body, and on the other, Christian theology which 'defines maternity only as an impossible elsewhere, a sacred beyond, a spiritual tie with the ineffable godhead and transcen-dence's ultimate support – necessarily virginal and committed to assumption . . . it establishes a sort of subject at the point where the subject and its speech split apart, fragment and vanish. Lay humanism took over the configuration of that subject through the cult of the mother; tenderness, love and seat of social conser-vation.'[36] In addition to her analysis of the cultural symbolism of motherhood, Kristeva also makes an identification between poetic impulses and a notion of 'feminine' flux and changeability.[37] The instability of poetic rhythms is related to the fluid impulses of the semiotic *chora* and its drives or energies, a network of rhythmic effects working within and between the signifying processes. The metaphoric alignment of the *chora* and an equivocal, undecidable conception of 'the feminine' is facilitated by the *chora*'s positioning prior to the rupture of entry into language (and so into the symbolic ordering of the Name of the Father). Kristeva states: 'The mother's body is therefore what mediates the symbolic law organising social relations and what becomes the ordering principle of the semiotic *chora*.'[38]

An affirmation of the poetic, musicalising, rhythmical aspect of language thus becomes equivalent to an affirmation of the feminine, facilitated by the cultural identification of the two aspects. Such an affirmation may be characterised as a kind of *jouissance* mediating between on the one hand schizophrenia (loss of control, delirium, excess) and on the other hand language as control, reason, communication. But this phase is apparently *still* contextualised by a 'feminine' force which is negative. This is because if 'the feminine' is equated with excess, *jouissance*, this loss of control becomes equivalent to a loss of creativity and an abandonment to madness. But, Kristeva argues, the constant *renewal* of the oscillation prevents this kind of determination and maintains it as a process.

The pre-Oedipal *chora* remains as a force which punctuates the symbolic. Kristeva takes up the Kleinian characterisation of this force as maternal, the oralising pulsion regenerating through and across the phallic economy.

Oralisation (is) a reunion with the mother's body which is no longer viewed as an engendering, hollow and vaginated, expelling and rejecting body, but rather as a vocalic one – throat, voice and breasts; music, rhythm, prosody, paragrams and the prophetic parabola.[39]

What emerges from Kristeva's activation of the maternal metaphor is not merely a valorisation of the 'feminine' side of language, the poetic and rhythmic 'secondary' aspect, but a subtle aspect of the alignment of creativity and production. In this sense the possibility of gesturing towards feminism's 'unknown' is made possible by the metaphor which, Kristeva writes, creates 'a surplus of meaning' which 'manages to open the surface of signs towards the unrepresentable'.[40] By taking up the metaphoric potentials of pregnancy and femininity it seems Nietzsche is able to effect a strategic parody of sexual difference. But such a parody is only possible on the basis of the return of those distinctions, albeit re-thought. It is a dangerous move to see the strategic, textual freedom of masks and changeability as a freedom from sexual difference. The space created apparently becomes an economy beyond conservation and limitation, a gift of the body which gives of the associative qualities of sexual difference to make them available in a general economy. This move apparently frees men and women to appropriate or open up strategies of sexual difference in a space of interchange.

But the space which is created is empty. It is not even a space, but annihilation, because it seeks neutrality. Nietzsche writes: 'if both partners felt impelled by love to renounce themselves, we should then get – I do not know what; perhaps an empty space?'[41]

To reintroduce sexual difference into the space may seem to reinstate the problem of differentially assigned values, and hence the problem of priority. Is sexual difference prior, or part of a more general economy? The decidability of this question is, for Derrida, a dubious project to work towards – the choice between the neutrality of Being or a biologically determined sexuality is no choice at all, if it implies there is a teleological 'truth' at the end to answer the question finally. However, this does not prevent the question being 'voiced', as Derrida writes. Neutralising the questions may lead to the systematic reincorporation of those voices under the (closed?) umbrella of patriarchy. Putting a question to Derrida, Christie McDonald asks:

What seems to be at stake as you take up Heidegger's reading of Nietzsche is whether or not sexual difference is 'a regional question in a larger order which would subordinate it first to the domain of a general ontology, subsequently to that of a fundamental ontology and finally to the question of the truth (whose?) of being itself'. You thereby question the status of the argument and at the same time the qustion itself.[42]

Derrida would not return a simple answer because to do so would, in his terms, simply reinstate either a fundamental essentialism or a notion of Being prior to sexuality. In putting binary differentiation into question, he must also put such an either/or solution into question. Hence the employment of 'feminine' metaphors may be exploitation, or it may open a general economy with radical implications, but to decide this question would necessitate returning to some of the criteria of truth and intentionality which have already been made problematic in the course of Derrida's texts and within feminism.

It seems 'the phase of reversal'[43] Derrida has referred to may make a space for women to reflect on the *implications* of using such metaphors. Derrida questions the will to a 'proper' body, a 'value of existence' attached to one figure above another, and adds a further question as to the status of a simple 'representative' model of the metaphor. Can the metaphor be seen as the sole criterion of exploitation or freedom? 'is it not difficult to recognise in the movement of this term a 'representation of women'? Furthermore, I do not know if it is to a change in representation that we should trust the future'[44] The metaphor of maternity attempts to name that which seems unnameable, and yet in this very gesture is contained the danger of its being incorporated into the terms of representation it is attempting to question. But, as Domna C. Stanton suggests, the dilemma requires constant attention to prevent the silence of the same. 'For either we name and become entrapped in the structure of the already named, or else we do not name and remain trapped in passivity, powerlessness and a perpetuation of the same.'[45]

The constant re-thinking of the space of the body, while it cannot dissolve difference, displaces it, and it is such a displacement which challenges phallocentrism. The enactment of the process, an active displacement, may prove to be an action not fully recuperable into phallocentric discourse. As part of such an action, the metaphor of maternity may not be reducible entirely to a relation of dominance – 'being *as*', 'Woman *as* mother' – but may express an attempt to give ear to the potentialities of other, surprising voices.

Notes

1 Friedrich Nietzsche, *Beyond Good and Evil, Prelude to a Philosophy of the Future*, trans. R.J. Hollingdale, Harmondsworth, Penguin, 1977, p.161. Henceforth *BGE*

2 Plato, *The Symposium*, trans. Stanley Rosen, New Haven, Yale University Press, 1968

3 'What I Owe the Ancients' *Twilight of the Idols or How to Philosophize with a Hammer*, trans. R.J. Hollingdale, Harmondsworth, Penguin, 1972, pp.105–11. Henceforth *TI*

4 *Thus Spoke Zarathustra, A Book for Everyone and No One*, trans. R.J. Hollingdale, Harmondsworth, Penguin, 968, p.91. Henceforth *TSZ*

5 *Daybreak, Thoughts on the Prejudices of Morality*, trans. R.J. Hollingdale, Cambridge University Press, p.223

6 *The Gay Science*, trans. Walter Kaufmann, New York, Vintage, 1974, p.317, n.93. Henceforth *GS*

7 For example, see Eva Figes, *Patriarchal Attitudes*, London, Virago, 1978, pp.127–9

8 Jacques Derrida, *Spurs/Eperons, Nietzsche's Styles/Les Styles de Nietzsche*, trans. Barbara Harlow, University of Chicago Press, 1979, p.67

9 *BGE*, p.13

10 Eric Blondel, 'Nietzsche: Life as Metaphor', David B. Allison (ed.), *The New Nietzsche*, London, MIT Press, 1985, p.162
11 'On Truth and Lie in an Ultra-Moral Sense', 1873
12 *BGE*, p.231
13 *Spurs*, p.95
14 Domna C. Stanton 'Difference on Trial: A Critique of the Maternal Metaphor in Cixous, Irigaray and Kristeva', in Nancy K. Miller (ed), *The Poetics of Gender*, Columbia University Press, 1986, p.158
15 *TI*, p.40–1
16 ibid., p.23
17 *GS*, p.167
18 *Spurs*, p.57
19 *GS*, p.137
20 *BGE*, p.69
21 Betsey Draine, 'Writing, Deconstruction and Other Unnatural Acts', Boundary 2, Spring/Fall 1981, vol.9 no.3/vol.10, no.1, pp.425–37
22 *TSZ*, 'For the woman the man is only the means; the end is always the child.' p.91
23 'Nietzsche contra Wagner', *The Portable Nietzsche*, (ed.) Walter Kaufmann, New York, Viking, 1954, p.682–3
24 *TI*, p.110
25 *GS*, p.129
26 *BGE*, p.161
27 *TSZ*, p.181
28 *Spurs*, p.77
29 ibid.
30 *TSZ*, p.301
31 ibid., p.244–7
32 Gayle L. Ormiston 'Traces of Derrida; Nietzsche's Image of Woman', *Philosophy Today*, Summer, 1984, pp.178–88
33 Principally taken up in the works of Helene Cixous, Luce Irigaray and Julia Kristeva.
34 For example, Simone de Beauvoir, *The Second Sex*, trans. H.M. Pashley, Harmondsworth, Penguin, 1984
35 Julia Kristeva, 'Stabat Mater', trans. Leon S. Roudiez, in Toril Moi (ed.), *The Kristeva Reader*, Oxford, Blackwell, 1986, p.161
36 'Motherhood According to Giovanni Bellini', trans. Thomas Gora, Alice Jardine and Leon S. Roudiez, in Leon S. Roudiez (ed.), *Desire in Language, a Semiotic Approach to Literature and Art*, Oxford, Blackwell, 1984, p.237
37 *Revolution in Poetic Language*, trans. Margaret Waller, Columbia University Press, 1984, Henceforth *RPL*
38 *RPL*, p.27
39 ibid., p.154
40 *Histoires d'amour*, Paris, Denoël, 1983, p.254, 344

41 *GS*, p.319
42 'Choreographies', *Diacritics*, no.12, 1982, p.66
43 Derrida writes: 'I strongly and repeatedly insist on the necessity of the phase of reversal, which people have perhaps too swiftly attempted to discredit . . . To neglect this phase of reversal is to forget that the structure of the opposition is one of conflict and subordination and this is to pass too swiftly . . . to a *neutralisation* which in *practice* leaves things in their former state.' *Positions*, trans. Alan Bass, London, Athlone Press, 1980, pp.56–7
44 'Choreographies', p.75
45 'Difference on Trial', p.164

· 8 ·

Foucault and Derrida on Nietzsche and the End(s) of 'Man'

ALAN D. SCHRIFT

I teach you the overman. Man is something that must be overcome. What have you done to overcome him?

NIETZSCHE

Does man really exist? To imagine, for an instant, what the world and thought and truth might be if man did not exist is considered to be merely indulging in paradox. This is because we are so blinded by the recent manifestation of man that we can no longer remember a time – and it is not so long ago – when the world, its order, and human beings existed, but man did not. It is easy to see why Nietzsche's thought should have had, and still has for us, such a disturbing power when it introduced in the form of an imminent event, the Promise-Threat, the notion that man would soon be no more – but would be replaced by the overman; in a philosophy of the Return, this meant that man had long since disappeared and would continue to disappear, and that our modern thought about man, our concern for him, our humanism, were all sleeping serenely over the threatening rumble of his non-existence.

FOUCAULT

The name of man being the name of that being who, throughout the history of metaphysics or of ontotheology – in other words, throughout his entire history – has dreamed of full presence, the reassuring foundation, the origin and the end of play.

DERRIDA

Approximately fifteen years after the appearance of Georges Bataille's influential *Sur Nietzsche*[1] and immediately following the publication of Heidegger's two-volume *Nietzsche* in 1961, a significant revival of interest in Nietzsche developed in French circles. The next two decades were to be marked by a virtual explosion of new approaches to Nietzsche interpretation. In 1962, Gilles Deleuze's *Nietzsche et la philosophie*[2] appeared. Two years later, an international colloquium on Nietzsche was held at Royaumont,[3] with such figures as Deleuze, Michel Foucault, Henri Birault, Jean Wahl, Gabriel Marcel, Jean Beaufret, and Karl Löwith in attendance. The next ten years saw books dealing exclusively or primarily with Nietzsche by, among others, Jean Granier, Maurice Blanchot, Pierre Klossowski, Jean-Michel Rey, Bernard Pautrat, Pierre Boudot, Sarah Kofman, and Paul Valadier;[4] special issues on Nietzsche by some of France's leading journals,[5] and a second major conference, at Cerisy-la-Salle in 1972, addressing the theme '*Nietzsche aujourd'hui*.'

This proliferation of Nietzsche interpretation in the 1960s and 1970s exhibits two of the basic trends of a new generation of French philosophers. First, these interpretations reflect the passage away from the preceding generation's preoccupation with Hegel, Husserl, and Heidegger. Although the 'three H's' continue to exert a great influence on contemporary French philosophy, the problems which engage this new generation are framed by another influential triumvirate: the 'masters of suspicion' – Nietzsche, Freud, and Marx. The second trend accompanies the first: a move away from the metaphysical humanism which characterized, for example, Sartre's existentialism, toward a new awareness of the subject as a function of discourse within the space of interpretation. It is this second trend, the subject as a function of interpretation rather than a privileged epistemological or metaphysical starting point, which I will examine in the following discussion of Foucault's and Derrida's readings of Nietzsche. Both Foucault and Derrida refuse to view Nietzsche as a figure within the tradition of philosophical anthropology and they refrain from viewing Nietzsche as a forerunner of the existentialists. Instead, they focus on, among other things, his critique of the foundations of metaphysical humanism and his initiating a deconstruction of the philosophical anthropological subject. In what follows, I shall examine their respective discussions of Nietzsche and the 'end' of 'man' and will attempt to show that their respective conclusions regarding the future of 'man' pick up on themes drawn from Nietzsche's critique of man, subjectivity, and authority. Moreover, I will argue that while their critical strategies appear on the surface to diverge, this divergence belies a basic similarity in their positions concerning the concept of subjectivity and the need for a critique of authority.

To begin, it will be helpful to survey briefly the general intellectual scene in which Foucault's and Derrida's readings of Nietzsche first appeared. In the early work of Michel Foucault, we find a typical enunciation of the connection between Nietzsche and three basic themes of contemporary French philosophy: the hermeneutics of suspicion; the reflection on the nature of language; and the end of 'man.' At the Seventh International Philosophical Colloquium at Royaumont in 1964, Foucault presented a paper entitled 'Nietzsche, Freud, Marx.'[6] In these three thinkers, Foucault locates a profound change in the nature of the sign and the manner in which signs in general can be interpreted. This change, which Foucault views as breaking the ground for the modern epoch,[7] involves a transformation from an emphasis on the representative function of the sign toward a view of the sign as already a part of the activity of interpretation. This is to say, signs are no longer viewed as the reservoir of some deep, hidden meaning; rather, they are surface phenomena, linked to an inexhaustible network which condemns interpretation to an infinite task:

Interpretation can never be brought to an end, simply because there is nothing to interpret. There is nothing absolutely primary to interpret because, at bottom, everything is already interpretation. Each sign is in itself not the thing that presents itself to interpretation, but the interpretation of other signs.[8]

In Marx's talk of phenomena as 'hieroglyphs,' Freud's view of the dream as always already an interpretation, and Nietzsche's theory of masks and the essential incompleteness of the interpretive act, Foucault locates a movement away from the 'hegemony of the sign' as a univocal relation between a signifier and a signified towards the properly *hermeneutical* view of the sign as always already interpreted and interpreting. It is in this sense that the hermeneut must be suspicious, for the naïve view of the sign as a simple relation of signifier and signified obscures relations of domination (Marx), neurotic desire (Freud), and decadence (Nietzsche).

This is the context in which Foucault issued his often quoted dictum that *'hermeneutics and semiology are two ferocious enemies.'*[9] What is not often mentioned in discussions of Foucault is that, in this context, it is the task of hermeneutics which is affirmed and that of semiology which is criticized. In the context of his remarks at Royaumont, Foucoult views 'semiology' as that investigation of signs which remains at the level of the structural transformations within language and which asserts the 'absolute existence of signs.' To hermeneutics, on the other hand, he assigns all inquiry into what these signs might signify, i.e., their 'meaning,' and in so doing he subordinates the absolute existence of signs to the infinite task of interpretation. We need not, at this point, become embroiled in the controversies over if and when Foucault renounced his approval of the hermeneutic enterprise. All that is required for our present purposes is to make explicit Nietzsche's inclusion, with Freud and Marx, at the forefront of the contemporary French scene.

The next two themes, the reflection on the nature of language and the dissolution of man, are both central motifs of the structuralist movement that became prominent in France concomitant with the renewed interest in Nietzsche. However, these two themes are not the exclusive concern of the structuralists: both are raised in Foucault's *The Order of Things*, a work in which he explicitly refuses to accept the structuralist label.[10] In this text, Nietzsche is singled out as the precursor of the *epistēmē* of the twentieth century, the *epistēmē* that erupted with the question of language as 'an enigmatic multiplicity that must be mastered.'[11] For Foucault, it was 'Nietzsche the philologist' who was 'the first to connect the philosophical task with a radical reflection upon language,'[12] and in so far as the question of the being of language is still the single most important question confronting the contemporary *epistēmē*, Foucault traces the roots of this *epistēmē* back to Nietzsche.

In much the same way, Foucault discovers in Nietzsche the first attempt at the dissolution of man:

Perhaps we should see the first attempt at this uprooting of Anthropology — to which, no doubt, contemporary thought is dedicated — in the

Nietzschean experience: by means of a philological critique, by means of a certain form of biologism, Nietzsche rediscovered the point at which man and God belong to one another, at which the death of the second is synonymous with the disappearance of the first, and at which the promise of the superman signifies first and foremost the imminence of the death of man.[13]

In speaking of the disappearance or the death of man, Foucault has something quite specific in mind, and it would not be misleading to view 'man' in this context as something of a technical term. 'Man' names for Foucault that 'strange empirico-transcendental doublet,' the analysis of whose 'actual experience' functions at the transcendental levels of the biological and historico-cultural conditions which make empirical knowledge possible. 'Man' is thus the being who serves to center the increasingly disorganized representations of the classical *epistēmē* and who, as such, comes to be the privileged object of philosophical anthropology.[14] The passage quoted above, relating Nietzsche to the uprooting of anthropology, follows by one page a reference to Kant's formulation of anthropology as the foundation of philosophy. In the *Critique of Pure Reason*, Kant discussed the three questions with which human reason is interested: What can I know? What must I do? What am I permitted to hope?[15] In his *Introduction to Logic*, we find these three perennial philosophical questions referred to a fourth: What is man? Of these four questions, Kant remarks:

The first question is answered by *Metaphysics*, the second by *Morals*, the third by *Religion*, and the fourth by *Anthropology*. In reality, however all these might be reckoned under anthropology, since the first three questions refer to the last.[16]

Within this reckoning, Foucault locates the birth of the discipline of philosophical anthropology.[17] The references to Nietzsche and to Kant appeared in a section entitled 'The Anthropological Sleep,' and it is clear that Foucault sees the modern *epistēmē* being awakened from its anthropological slumber by Nietzsche in much the same way as Kant saw himself awakened from his own dogmatic slumber by Hume.[18] Only by understanding Foucault's talk of 'man' as designating a foundational concept of Kantian anthropology can we make sense of his saying that 'man is a recent invention, a figure not yet two centuries old.'[19]

While this foundational concept has been privileged in the discourse of the human sciences since Kant, Foucault foresees the end of man's reign as such a foundation. It is the announcement of this end that he locates in Nietzsche's doctrine of the overman, for the overman will overcome nihilism only by overcoming humanity. This point is crucial for understanding Foucault's situating Nietzsche at the beginning of the end of man. For Foucault, Nietzsche offers us a philosophy of the future, and that future will belong not to man but to the overman. Thus the overman makes his appearance in Nietzsche together with the 'last man:' both are introduced for the first time in Zarathustra's 'Prologue.'[20] This last man is literally the last of man, and the overman is here interpreted as a completely different 'species,' as something no-longer-man. With this in mind, we can understand the significance of Foucault's final reference to Nietzsche in *The Order of Things*, in which he couples Nietzsche's death of God with the death of man.[21] Viewing Foucault's 'death of man' in Nietzschean terminology, we find the death of man to be the death of the 'last man,' the death of the murderer of God. Foucault here recalls that in *Thus Spoke Zarathustra* ('The Ugliest Man'), God is reported to have died of pity upon encountering the last man, and he writes:

Rather than the death of God – or, rather, in the wake of that death and in profound correlation with it – what Nietzsche's thought heralds is the end of his murderer; it is the explosion of man's face in laughter, and the return of masks; it is the scattering of the profound stream of time by which he felt himself carried along and whose pressure he suspected in the very being of things; it is the identity of the Return of the Same with the absolute dispersion of man.[22]

This is to say, Nietzsche's announcement of the disappearance of man as the standard-bearer of an all-too-serious anthropocentrism is applauded by Foucault for opening the post-modern *epistēmē*, one that henceforth will refrain from viewing man as the privileged center of representational thinking and discourse. And with Nietzsche's dispersion of man, Foucault locates a return of the project of a unification of language. The conclusion of Foucault's archaeological project in *The Order of Things* is thus inscribed within Nietzsche's eternal recurrence of the same – what recurs is the problem of language as a multiplicity to be mastered.

Whereas the classical *epistēmē* had unified language around the function of representation, the modern *epistēmē* left language as a disorganized fund to be utilized by the human subject for the purposes of meaningful expression. With the death of this subject, the question of the 'being' and 'unity' of language is once again posed. The past two decades of French philosophy can to a large extent be viewed as an inquiry into the implications for the 'human sciences' of the return of this question.

Let us now turn from Foucault's inscription of the death of man in the eternal recurrence of the question of the being of language to the texts of Jacques Derrida. In Derrida's texts we find an uncanny consistency as regards Nietzsche's appearance. In general, Derrida 'uses' Nietzsche's texts as a paradigm of undecidability that frustrates the logocentric longing to choose between one or the other alternative within some sort of binary opposition.[23] A case in point is Derrida's 1968 lecture, 'The Ends of Man.' At the conclusion of this lecture, Derrida brings the undecidable logic of supplementarity to the two strategies that have appeared in connection with the deconstruction of metaphysical humanism. The first strategy proceeds by means of a return to the origins of the metaphysical tradition and uses the resources of this tradition against itself. In adopting this strategy, 'one risks ceaselessly confirming, consolidating, relieving [*relève*] at an always more certain depth that which one allegedly deconstructs.'[24] The second deconstructive strategy affirms an absolute break with tradition, seeking to change ground in a discontinuous and irruptive fashion. However, such a strategy fails to recognize that one cannot break with the tradition while retaining its language. The inevitable consequence of this blindness to the powers of language is a naïve reinstatement of a 'new' ground on the very site one sought to displace.

According to Derrida, the first of these styles of deconstruction is that of Heidegger, while the second is the style that currently prevails in France. (I might add that we have seen this second strategy in our discussion of Foucault's *The Order of Things*.) In the application of these deconstructive strategies to Nietzsche and the 'end of man,' two very different interpretations result. For Heidegger, Nietzsche emerges as the last great metaphysician, in whose writings the end of man appears as the culmination of metaphysical voluntarism. Overman, as pure will, thus for

Heidegger assumes the form of a metaphysical repetition of humanism. For Foucault, Nietzsche emerges as the first break from the modern *epistēmē*, and the end of man appears in the overman's laughter at the going-under of the last man.

Derrida warns that we must refrain from choosing one strategy rather than the other. The two strategies supplement one another, and we are now at a point in history where there is no question of a simple choice between them. In other words, we must choose *both at once*, thereby effecting a change of ground while returning to the origins. To do so is to effect a change of *style* in philosophical writing. Derrida marks this change of style when he confronts Nietzsche's position on the 'end of man.' He finds Nietzsche's position equivocal – that is, there is more than one 'end of man' in Nietzsche. To read Nietzsche's texts requires that we be prepared for multiple readings, and there are in fact *two* ends of man: the end as *eschaton* and the end as *telos*. Nietzsche confronts us with this equivocal end of man at the conclusion of *Zarathustra*, where we find (the last) man meeting his end in the choice between the higher man [*höherer Mensch*] and the overman [*Übermensch*]. This equivocation on the end of man points to Derrida's own view of the undecidable place of the subject within philosophical discourse. Unlike Heidegger and the Foucault of *The Order of Things*, Derrida refuses to do away with the subject. Instead, he seeks to situate the subject. As he puts it – admittedly in a different context – 'I believe that at a certain level both of experience and of philosophical and scientific discourse, one cannot get along without the notion of the subject. It is a question of knowing where it comes from and how it functions.'[25]

To provide an answer to the question of the situation of the subject in deconstruction, I would suggest that we return to Nietzsche's text and examine his attempt to deconstruct his own subjectivity as an author. In this Preface to the second edition of *Daybreak*, Nietzsche remarks that 'in the face of any authority, one is not *allowed* to think, [instead] one has to – *obey*!' In so far as the author has come to occupy a position of authority within the traditional view of interpretation, we should not be surprised to find in his affirmation of the *activity* of interpretation that Nietzsche expresses an antipathy to any factor, including the author that tends to inhibit this activity and limit its play. Throughout the two volumes of *Human, All-too-Human*, Nietzsche cautions against confusing the work with its author. Once the text has been written, it lives a life of its own, and by bringing the text into the public domain the author relinquishes all authority over what it is to mean: 'When his book opens its mouth, the author must shut his.'[26]

Throughout his writings, Nietzsche continues to question the privileged position of the author within the space of interpretation and in the third chapter of *Ecce Homo*, entitled 'Why I Write Such Good Books,' he openly acknowledges and affirms the consequences of the self-deconstruction of his own literary author(ity). In the opening sentence, Nietzsche separates himself from his texts: 'I am one thing, my writings are another.'[27] From here he proceeds to confront the question of 'being undersood or *not* understood.' In the pages that follow we find Nietzsche proudly proclaiming a number of reasons for his writings' not being understood, reasons that reflect the problematic relation of the author to his text. To understand Nietzsche's writings as Nietzsche understands them, one would have to be Nietzsche:

Ultimately, nobody can get more out of things, including books, than he already knows. For what one lacks access to from experience one will have no ear. Now, let us imagine an extreme case: that a book speaks of nothing but events that lie altogether beyond the possibility of any frequent or even rare experience – that it is the *first* language for a new series of experiences. In that case, simply nothing will be heard, but there will be the acoustic illusion that where nothing is heard, *nothing is there*.[28]

This extreme position indicates that there are different ways in which one's writings are not understood. Granted Nietzsche's perspectivism, no one could possibly understand his text as he does. Yet such an understanding would not, in his view, even be desirable. One might recall here Zarathustra's remark to his followers:

An experimenting and questioning was my every move; – and verily, one must also *learn* to answer such questioning: That however – is my taste: – not good, not bad, but *my* taste of which I am no longer ashamed and which I have no wish to hide. 'This – is *my* way, – where is yours?' thus I answered those who asked me 'the way.' For *the* way, that does not exist.[29]

Nietzsche does not lament the lack of an identical reproduction of meaning in his readers. Instead, he takes pride in the fact that his contemporary readers 'lack the ears' to hear what speaks within his text and he absolves himself of responsibility for having caught no fish with the bait his writings set out.[30] To be caught by Nietzsche's fish hooks, to experience his writings in the affirmative sense, would result in the reader's being incited to act, to take action toward a transvaluation of values. This does not mean that one will duplicate the Nietzschean transvaluation. Rather, having sufficient style to respond to the call to transvalue values, Nietzsche extends to his readers the creative freedom to bring their own perspectives to the task of transvaluation. We find in this discussion a transvalued sense of textual communication. That is to say, communication is not the direct transmission of meaning or truth between individuals or between text and reader. Rather, one communicates an attitude, a stance, a *style* that is transformed in the process of perspectival appropriation. As an author, Nietzsche thus relinquishes his position of authority in favor of a position more conducive to provoking healthy performative responses on the part of his readers. In the concluding section of *Beyond Good and Evil*, one finds Nietzsche expressing a fear that his writings are becoming truths. The reason for Nietzsche's concern is that the communication of truth runs counter to his conception of his function as an author in so far as all truths, including his own, if they are accepted *as* truths, can only serve to inhibit the healthy response of transvaluation his writings seek to 'communicate.'

Nietzsche's self-deconstruction of his own authorial-authoritarian subjectivity provides the link between his critique of the traditional view of interpretation and the critique of the philosophical subject. In emphasizing the dynamic character of the interpretive process, Nietzsche rejects the view of interpretation as a relationship between a subject and an object. For Nietzsche, both 'subject' and 'object' are themselves already interpretations,[31] and when he writes that 'one may not ask: "who then interprets?"'[32] it is only because such a question already mislocates the process of interpretation. Likewise, one may not ask 'what then is interpreted?' Interpretation is not grounded in either the subject or the object; it exists in the *between*, in the space that separates them. Within this space, subject and object can function only as limits, and the attempt to focus the interpretive process in the direction of either will serve only to obscure the dynamics of this process and put an end to its proliferating play.[33]

With this question of the 'identity' of the author of the Nietzschean text, we return, do we not, to the essential Nietzschean question raised by Foucault: 'who is speaking?'[34] In the final section of my paper, I would like to sketch both Foucault's and Derrida's response to this Nietzschean question. Moreover, I would like to suggest that while they respond in different ways, their respective answers pick up a thread already woven into the Nietzschean text. Foucault raises his question on two occasions. It appears first in *The Order of Things* in the context of Foucault's crediting Nietzsche for opening up language as 'an enigmatic multiplicity that must be mastered.' Foucault writes:

For Nietzsche, it was not a matter of knowing what good and evil were in themselves, but of who was being designated, or rather *who was speaking* when one said *Agathos* to designate oneself or *Deilos* to designate others. For it is there, in the *holder* of the discourse and, more profoundly still, in the *possessor* of the word, that language is gathered together in its entirety.[35]

How does Foucault respond to this Nietzschean question of 'who is speaking?' We can find an outline of Foucault's response previewed in the following remark from Nietzsche's *Nachlass*:

We see: an authority speaks – who speaks? – One may forgive human pride if it sought to make this authority as high as possible in order to feel as little humiliated as possible under it. Therefore – God speaks!

One needed God as an unconditional sanction, with no court of appeal, as a 'categorical imperative' – or, if one believed in the authority of reason, one needed a metaphysic of unity, by virtue of which this was logical.

Now suppose that belief in God has vanished: the question presents itself anew: 'who speaks?' – My answer, taken not from metaphysics but from animal physiology: *the herd instinct speaks*. It wants to be master: hence its '*thou shalt*!' – it will allow value to the individual only from the point of view of the whole, for the sake of the whole, it hates those who detach themselves – it turns the hatred of all individuals against them.[36]

We find in Nietzsche's remark that *authority* speaks, first the authority of God and then the authority of the herd. We have already seen that Foucault links the disappearance of man with the death of God. Nietzsche's overman, who heralds the demise of God and the last/herd man, will be subject to no authority and, inasmuch as both divine and human subjectivity function within a network of relations of power, authority and submission, the overman will not be a subject to all. Foucault links the subject and subjection. In an essay written not long before his death, he writes:

> It is a form of power that makes individuals subjects. There are two meanings of the word *subject*: subject to someone else by control and dependence, and tied to his own identity by a conscience or self-knowledge. Both meanings suggst a form of power which subjugates and makes subject to.[37]

The subject appears to Foucault as an ideological product, a functional principle of discourse rather than its privileged origin. This is not to say that the subject is to be entirely abandoned, but that its authority may be deconstructed. It is a matter of depriving the subject of its role as originator and analysing the subject as a variable and complex function of discourse and power:

> We should suspend the typical questions: how does a free subject penetrate the density of things and endow them with meaning; how does it accomplish its design by animating the rules of discourse from within? Rather, we should ask: under what conditions and through what forms can an entity like the subject appear in the order of discourse; what position does it occupy; what functions does it exhibit; and what rules does it follow in each type of discourse?[38]

Foucault here returns to a suggestion he made five years earlier at Royaumont. In his concluding remarks on the obligation of interpretation to interpret itself to infinity, he notes:

> . . . interpretation will be henceforth always interpretation by the 'who?': one does not interpret what there is in the signified, but one interprets, fundamentally, *who* has posed the interpretation. The origin [*principe*] of interpretation is nothing other than the interpreter, and this is perhaps the sense that Nietzsche gave to the word 'psychology.'[39]

However, to ask '*who* interprets?' or '*who* speaks?' is not to expect as an answer the name of a subject. Foucault makes this clear at the conclusion of his essay 'What is an Author?' when he claims that the question 'who is speaking?' must give way to the question 'what difference does it make who is speaking?' Rather, the question 'who?' is inscribed within 'psychology,' understood by Nietzsche in *Beyond Good and Evil* as 'morphology and *the doctrine of the development of the will to power.*'[40] It is the will to power that speaks and interprets, not a 'subject,' and the question 'who?' calls for a genealogical inquiry into the type of force (life-affirming or life-negating) that manifests itself in speech or interpretation. The subject, Nietzsche tells us, is itself an interpretation, a created entity, a 'simplification with the object of defining the force that posits, invents, thinks.'[41] Inasmuch as something is defined for the purposes of making it more *manageable*, Nietzsche, like Foucault, recognizes the oppressive use which can be made of the principle of subjectivity as a principle of domination. As Nietzsche makes clear, for example, in his tracing the genealogy of 'free will' to the 'hangman's metaphysics' of Christianity, individuality and subjectivity can and have been used for the purposes of subjection to the will, law or authority of another. The overman will not be, strictly speaking, a subject at all. He will be a conglomeration of forces, an amalgam of will to power. He will not exercize authority, nor will he be appealed to as an authority.

Yet there is another answer to the question 'who is speaking?', one that adopts a different strategy in attacking the classical concept of the subject, and this, I believe, is the response offered by Derrida. Like Foucault, Derrida is also sensitive to the authoritarian domination within the classical concept of the subject. But his strategy in decentering the subject as a privileged center of discourse is not as overtly political as that of Foucault. Instead, he focuses his deconstructive critique on *literary* authority. And when Derrida, in *Of Grammatology*, deconstructs the writer as a sovereign subject in command of the reserve within language, or when he fractures the 'subject of writing' in his discussions of Freud, a Nietzschean 'subject' emerges. The classical subject, as a privileged center, thus disappears within the system of relations which is writing [*écriture*]:

> The 'subject' of writing does not exist if we mean by that some sovereign solitude of the author. The subject of writing is a *system* of relations between strata: the Mystic Pad, the psyche, society, the world.[42]

In dispersing the subject within a system of textual relations,

Derrida adopts a Nietzschean strategy of refusing to hypostasize the subject. For Nietzsche, the refusal is grounded in a philosophy of will to power as active force within the infinite play of becoming. For Derrida, the refusal is grounded in a theory of textuality and the view that the person writing or reading is always already inscribed in a textual network that cannot and will not be dominated absolutely.

What links these two refusals is the emphasis on fluidity of relations, as both Nietzsche and Derrida view the classical concept of the subject as functioning in a way which engenders separation and fixation. In Nietzsche's case, it is the play of relations of forces and the accumulation of power within this play that is blocked by the hypostasization of the subject: the concept of the subject performs only a *preservative* function and to enhance one's life within the innocent, infinite play of becoming, one must refrain from conceiving of the subject as a static, enduring substance. In Derrida's case, it is the relational 'system' of writing/play that resists the classical notion of a subjectivity which functions as a center and limit to this play/writing. For Derrida, it is Nietzsche who has pointed the way to an affirmation of the decentered play of writing that disrupts the metaphysics of presence which guides the logocentric tradition. Of Nietzsche's affirmation Derrida says that it is:

the joyous affirmation of the play of the world and of the innocence of becoming, the affirmation of a world of signs without fault, without truth, and without origin which is offered to an active interpretation. *This affirmation then determines the noncenter otherwise than as loss of the center.* And it plays without security, [surrendering] itself to *genetic* indetermination, to the *seminal* adventure of the trace.

Derrida then provides the final link which brings us to our conclusion. Nietzsche's affirmation:

which is no longer turned toward the origin, affirms play and tries to pass beyond man and humanism, the name of man being the name of that being who, throughout the history of metaphysics or of ontotheology – in other words, throughout his entire history – has dreamed of full presence, the reassuring foundation, the origin and the end of play.[43]

Grammatology, the 'science' of writing, will not be a science of man. 'Man', the name bestowed on the subject as center, as the full presence of consciousness in being, must be decentered if there is to be a logic of the *grammē* – 'man' must be deconstructed, must be allowed to play. In Derrida's call for play we can hear the echo of Zarathustra's message to the higher men in the fourth book of *Thus Spoke Zarathustra*, in which the recurrent theme is the invitation to learn to dance and laugh:

> You higher men, the worst about you is that all of you have not learned to dance as one must dance – dancing away over yourselves! What does it matter that you are failures? How much is still possible! So *learn* to laugh away over yourselves! Lift up your hearts, you good dancers, high, higher! And do not forget good laughter. This crown of him who laughs, this rose-wreath crown: to you, my brothers, I throw this crown. Laughter I have pronounced holy; you higher men, *learn* to laugh![44]

The common appeal to a Nietzschean critique of authority suggests that the differences between the Foucauldian and Derridean projects may be best viewed in terms of a difference in regional application rather than a fundamental distinction in philosophical orientation. Yet we should not overlook an important rhetorical distinction regarding their respective pronouncements on the future of 'man.' This distinction turns on a difference between the language of 'ends' and the language of 'closure.' Whereas Foucault speaks of the 'end' of man accompanying the birth of a new *epistēmē*, Derrida refuses to adopt this apocalyptic tone, speaking instead of the closure of man within the metaphysics of presence. This difference in tone itself bears on their respective readings of the future of man in Nietzsche. There are two 'men' whose future will give way to the overman – the last man and the higher man – and while Foucault focuses on the former, Derrida appears to address the future of the latter. Foucault thus speaks of the 'end' of the last man – the end of the philosophical subject as the locus of subjection and subjugation – which will accompany the emergence of the over-man. Derrida, on the contrary, seems to indicate a closure of subjectivity – the limits of which can be marked by a 'certain laughter'[45] but from which absolute escape is impossible. On this point, Derrida may perhaps be acknowledging Zarathustra's 'dreadful' realization, in 'The Convalescent', that even the smallest man will recur eternally. In light of Zarathustra's own concession, Derrida refuses to speak of an 'end' of man. Nevertheless, man's future will be different as he escapes from the authoritarian limitations of a centered subjectivity, just as Nietzsche's higher man will be transformed when he learns to laugh and dance away over himself.

Before closing, however, I should add that Foucault himself moved away from the provocative rhetoric of the 'end' of man in his last work. Perhaps recognizing that he had become too caught up in the structuralist project of the 'death of the subject,' Foucault characterized the objective of his work over the last twenty years as an attempt 'to create a history of the different modes by which, in our culture, human beings are made subjects.'[46] The 'subject' is viewed here as a particular form of individuation, one that is a product of the power relations instituted in the modern Western state. Foucault thus defined his task in 1981 as promoting 'new forms of subjectivity through the refusal of this kind of individuality which has been imposed on us for several centuries.'[47]

Neither Foucault nor Derrida can sketch in great detail what this new being whose emergence they announce will look like, any more than Nietzsche could give us a detailed account of the being of the overman. Yet it is important to recognize that their critiques of metaphysical humanism do not result in an *anti-humanism*. As Derrida says with respect to the Heideggerian project of overcoming meaphysics, 'if the form of opposition and the oppositional structure are themselves metaphysical, then the relation of metaphysics to its other can no longer be one of opposition.'[48] Nietzsche's, Derrida's and Foucault's rejection of the subject or man will not take the form of an anti-humanism, for both humanism and anti-humanism remain within the same binary metaphysics and confront the same dilemmas. In appealing to Nietzsche and the end(s) of 'man', Derrida and Foucault indicate means of escape – or temporary leave – from the closure of metaphysical humanism by sketching a form of human being based on multiplicity, play and difference, rather than the traditional humanistic/logocentric values of subjectivity, consciousness, autonomy and self-identity. In so doing, they reveal both their indebtedness to Nietzsche's thinking and their place in the history of philosophy as two of the 'philosophers of the future' to whom Nietzsche's writings were addressed.[49]

Notes

1 Georges Bataille, *Sur Nietzsche*, Paris, Gallimard, 1945
2 Gilles Deleuze, *Nietzsche et la philosophie*, Paris, Presses Universitaires de France, 1962; English translation by Hugh Tomlinson, *Nietzsche and Philosophy*, New York, Columbia University Press, 1983
3 The addresses and discussions at the colloquium, held July 4–8, 1964, were published as *Nietzsche: Cahiers du Royaumont*, Philosophie No. VI, Paris, Éditions de Minuit, 1967
4 Jean Granier, *La problème de la Vérité dans la philosophie de Nietzsche*, Paris, Éditions du Seuil, 1966; Maurice Blanchot, *L'Entretien infini*, Paris, Gallimard, 1969; Pierre Klossowski, *Nietzsche et le Cercle Vicieux*, Paris, Mercure de France, 1969 (Klossowski also translated Heidegger's two-volume *Nietzsche* for publication by Gallimard in 1971); Jean-Michel Rey, *L'enjeu des signes. Lecture de Nietzsche*, Paris, Éditions du Seuil, 1971; Bernard Pautrat, *Versions du soleil. Figures et système de Nietzsche*, Paris, Éditions du Seuil, 1971; Pierre Boudot, *L'ontologie de Nietzsche*, Paris, Presses Universitaires de France, 1971; Sarah Kofman, *Nietzsche et la métaphore*, Paris, Payot, 1972; Paul Valadier, *Nietzsche et la critique du christianisme*, Paris, Éditions du Cerf, 1974.
5 See, for example, *Poétique*, Vol. V, 1971 on 'Rhétorique et philosophie'; *Revue Philosophique*, No. 3, 1971 on 'Nietzsche'; *Critique*, no.313, 1973 on 'Lectures de Nietzsche'.
6 Reprinted in *Nietzsche: Cahiers du Royaumont*, pp.183–200; English translation by Alan D. Schrift forthcoming in *Hermeneutics and Postmodern Theories of Interpretation*, edition by Alan D. Schrift and Gayle L. Ormiston, Albany, State Unviersity of New York Press.
7 A similar view is advanced by Paul Ricoeur. See *Freud and Philosophy: An Essay on Interpretation*, translated by Denis Savage, New Haven, Yale University Press, 1970, pp.32–35; see also 'The Critique of Religion', translated by R. Bradley DeFord in *The Philosophy of Paul Ricoeur*, edited by Charles E. Reagan and David Steward, Boston, Beacon Press, 1978, pp.213–222.
8 Michel Foucault, 'Nietzsche, Freud, Marx' in *Nietzsche: Cahiers du Royaumont*, p.189. Unless otherwise noted, the translations from this text as well as the other French and German texts cited are my own.
9 Foucault, 'Nietzsche, Freud, Marx,' p.192
10 See, for example, the following remark which Foucault included in his foreword to the English edition of *The Order of Things*, New York, Random House, Inc., 1973, p.xiv: 'In France, certain half-witted "commentators" persist in labelling me a "structuralist." I have been unable to get it into their tiny minds that I have used none of the methods, concepts, or key terms that characterize structural analysis.'
11 Foucault, *The Order of Things*, p.305

12 Ibid., p.305
13 Ibid., p.342
14 Ibid., pp.313–321
15 Immanuel Kant, *Critique of Pure Reason*, A804, B832f
16 Immanuel Kant, *Kant's Introduction to Logic*, translated by T.K. Abbott, New York, Philosophical Lbrary, 1963, p.15
17 Heidegger makes a similar point when he discusses Kant's laying the foundation of metaphysics as philosophical anthropology; see Martin Heidegger, *Kant and the Problem of Metaphysics*, translated by James S. Churchill, Bloomington, Indiana University Press, 1962, pp.213–215
18 See Immanuel Kant's Introduction to the *Prolegomena to Any Future Metaphysics*.
19 Foucault, *The Order of Things*, p.xxiii; see also pp.308, 386–387. Kant's *Logic* was first published in 1800.
20 'The antithesis of the *overman* is the *last man*: I created him conjointly with the former.' Friedrich Nietzsche, *Werke. Kritische Gesamtausgabe*, edited by Giorgio Colli and Mazzino Montinari, Berlin, Walter de Gruyter, 167ff, Abt. VII, Bd. 1: 4[171].
21 Gilles Deleuze makes a similar point, coupling the death of God with the dissolution of the Self, in *Différence et répétition*, Paris, Presses Universitaires de France, 1968, pp.81ff. Deleuze there credits Klossowski for having first made this connection in 'Nietzsche, le polythéisme et la parodie', reprinted in *Un si funeste désir*, Paris, Gallimard, 1963.
22 Foucault, *The Order of Things*, p.385
23 I have discussed the similarities between Nietzsche's and Derrida's critiques of binary, oppositonal thinking elsewhere; see 'Genealogy and/as Deconstruction: Nietzsche, Derrida and Foucault on Philosophy as Critique' in *Postmodernism and Continental Philosophy*, edited by Hugh J. Silverman and Donn Welton, Albany, State University of New York Press, 1987.
24 Jacques Derrida, *Margins of Philosophy*, translated by Alan Bass, Chicago, University of Chicago Press, 1983, p.135 (translation altered)
25 Jacques Derrida, from the discussion following 'Structure, Sign, and Play in the Discourse of the Human Sciences' in *The Structuralist Controversy*, edited by Richard Macksey and Eugenio Donato, Baltimore, Johns Hopkins University Press, 1970, p.271
26 Nietzsche, *Assorted Opinions and Maxims*, section 140; cf. section 157; *MA*, sections 197, 208
27 *EH*, 'Why I Write Such Good Books', section 1
28 Ibid.
29 *ASZ* III, 'On the Spirit of Gravity', section 2
30 Cf. *EH*, *JGB*, section 1: 'From this moment forward all my writings are fish hooks: perhaps I understand how to fish as well as

anyone? . . . If nothing was *caught*, I am not to blame. *The fish were missing . . .* '

31 Cf. *WM*, section 481

32 *WM*, section 556

33 Derrida recognizes this point when he writes in *Spurs* that Nietzsche inaugurates the 'epochal regime of quotation marks which is to be enforced for every concept belonging to the system of philosophical decidability.' (Jacques Derrida, *Spurs: Nietzsche's Styles*, translated by Barbara Harlow, Chicago, University of Chicago Press, 1978, p.107.) This regime, which for Derrida disqualifies the hermeneutical project of deciphering the true sense of the text, frees reading from meaning, truth, being and presence. It also frees reading from the authority of the author and, in so doing, opens the text to an infinite play of interpretation. In *Spurs*, Derrida displays this epochal regime in his discussion of the forgotten umbrella, which I discuss at length elsewhere; see Schrift, 'Reading Derrida Reading Heidegger Reading Nietzsche' in *Research on Phenomenology*, Vol. XIV, 1984, pp.87–119.

34 Foucault addresses this question in *The Order of Things*, p.305; see also the conclusion of 'What is an Author?' in *Language, Counter-Memory, Practice*, translated by Donald F. Bouchard and Sherry Simon, Ithaca, Cornell University press, 1977, pp.137–138.

35 Foucault, *The Order of Things*, p.305

36 *WM*, section 275

37 Michel Foucault, 'Why Study Power: The Question of the Subject' in Hubert L. Dreyfus and Paul Rabinow, *Michel Foucault: Beyond Structuralism and Hermeneutics*, Chicago, University of Chicago Press, 1981, p.212

38 Foucault, 'What is an Author?', p.137–138

39 Foucault, 'Nietzsche, Freud, Marx', pp.191–92

40 *JGB*, section 23

41 *WM*, section 556

42 Jacques Derrida, *Writing and Difference*, translated by Alan Bass, Chicago, University of Chicago Press, 1978, pp.226–227

43 Ibid., p.292

44 *ASZ* IV, 'On the Higher Man', section 20

45 Cf. Derrida, *Writing and Difference*, pp.252–253

46 Foucault, 'Why Study Power: The Question of the Subject', p.208

47 Ibid., p.216

48 Derrida, *Spurs*, pp.117–19

49 This paper was first presented in July, 1984 at the Warwick Workshop in Continental Philosophy. I would like to thank David Wood for inviting me to participate in the workshop; I would also like to thank David Farrell Krell for his suggestions, both stylistic and substantive.

· 9 ·

Nietzsche on the
Edge of Town:
Deleuze and Reflexivity

HUGH TOMLINSON

The topic of this paper is *Nietzsche and Philosophy*[1] – and in particular the vulnerability of Gilles Deleuze's account of Nietzsche to reflexive attack. It was, says Sarah Kofman, Gilles Deleuze who restored to Nietzsche the freedom of the city of philosophy.[2] Nevertheless, it has proved difficult to settle him down to the sedentary life within its gates. Just what kind of citizen is the Nietzsche that Deleuze invents for us? How is Deleuze's 'recommendation for citizenship' to be read?

The title of Deleuze's book immediately directs us to the central problem for philosophers reading Nietzsche: his relationship to philosophy. The question is not the usual one of 'what is Nietzsche's philosophy?' but the more fundamental 'does it make sense to speak of Nietzsche and philosophy?' This is so for two reasons. First, Nietzsche's style does not fit easily into the traditional categories of philosophical writing. As Paul de Man says, we are faced with the 'patent literariness of texts that keep making claims usually associated with philosophy rather than literature'.[3] Secondly, and more importantly, Nietzsche's work itself calls radically into question the whole idea of philosophy as the sovereign discourse of truth. Nietzsche turns philosophy back on itself and exposes and encourages its inevitable self-undermining. It is Nietzsche who places the problem of reflexivity at the centre of philosophy. If his own views are taken seriously the place and status of philosophy itself becomes deeply problematic.

The philosophical reader of Nietzsche's work has two obvious hermeneutic strategies. The first involves the claim that, despite himself, Nietzsche was a traditional philosopher all along. The second, by contrast, involves accepting Nietzsche's own assessment of his relationship with philosophy and, as a result, affirming and adopting the radical reflexive thrust of his work. I will call these the 'traditional' and the 'reflexive' strategies. Although each strategy allows undecidably many specific 'readings of Nietzsche', there are important and fundamental differences between the two. Those who adopt the first strategy seek a 'deep order' beneath the 'superficial inconsistencies' of Nietzsche's texts. A 'Nietzschean system' is reconstructed from the fragments of his writings and placed alongside the work of the 'great philosophers' of the tradition. This strategy is favoured by many Anglo-Saxon commentators.[4] The second strategy involves showing that, whatever 'truths' and 'fragments for a system' Nietzsche apparently advances, these are always 'taken away' elsewhere, exposed as temporary coagulations in the flux of language. This is the strategy of Derrida and de Man.[5]

The paradox of Deleuze's reading of Nietzsche is that this radical 'philosopher of difference' appears to be following the first, i.e., the traditional, strategy. He does not concern himself with the dilemmas, twists and turns of 'reflexive' interpretation, but appears simply to assume that Nietzsche's work contains a 'system', which he proceeds to set out with unadorned directness. The first sentence of the book tells us that 'Nietzsche's most general project is the introduction of the concepts of sense and value into philosophy.'[6] The sense of something is dependent on the forces that take possession of it. These are revealed to interpretation as being of two qualitatively different types: active and reactive. Active forces are dominant and go to the limit of what they can do. Reactive forces are dominated and seek to separate active forces from what they can do. The value of something depends on the type of will power it expresses: will to power being the differential element from which forces derive, 'the genealogical element which determines the relation of force with force and produces their quality'.[7] Two primordial qualities are ascribed to the will to power: affirmation and negation. These are more profound than the qualities of forces that derive from them:[8]

they are immediate qualities of becoming itself. 'Affirmation is not action, but the power of becoming active, *becoming active* personified. Negation is not simple reaction but a *becoming reactive*.'[9] The will to power makes active forces affirm their difference from reactive forces; 'in them affirmation is primary, negation is only ever a consequence'.[10] In contrast, reactive forces begin by being opposed to what they are not, 'in them negation is primary'.[11] The formula of the active, strong man, 'I am good, therefore, you are evil', is distinguished from that of the weak, reactive man, 'You are evil, therefore I am good.'[12]

According to Deleuze, Nietzsche's philosophy is organised along the two great axes of force and power.[13] The typology of forces is seen as enabling Nietzsche to describe in detail the stages of human history as the history of the triumph of reactive forces.[14] Post-history is reached when the alliance between reactive forces and negation is broken and negation goes over to the side of affirmation and becomes active negation.[15] Active negation is the state of strong spirits which destroy the reactive in themselves, submitting it to the test of the eternal return.[16] This is the point of 'transmutation' of the 'transvaluation of all values'.

This, in briefest outline, is Deleuze's account of a Nietzschean system. At first sight it appears to be a 'philosophical system' of the traditional kind. But the crucial reflexive question which Nietzsche himself has taught us cannot be avoided: what happens when this system is 'applied to itself', how can it account for its own status? In order to expand this question it is useful to consider Deleuze's own account of the relationship between Nietzsche's 'thought' and traditional philosophy. Deleuze's Nietzsche replaces the old metaphysics, the philosophy of being, with the philosophy of the will. Creation and joy are the main principles of this philosophy. These are to be understood as critical principles: 'The typology of forces and the doctrine of the will to power are inseparable, in turn, from a critique which can be used to determine the genealogy of values, their nobility and baseness.'[17] The overall enterprise is that of critique, for 'Philosophy is at its most positive as critique, as an enterprise of demystification.'[18] It sets out to expose all the mystifications, all the fictions which enable reactive forces to prevail.[19] This is because 'Nietzsche thinks that the idea of critique is identical to that of philosophy.'[20] Kant's critique was a false one because he saw it as 'a force which should be brought to bear on all claims to knowledge and truth, but not on knowledge and truth themselves'.[21] The point of Nietzsche's critique 'is not justification but a different way of feeling: another sensibility'.[22] This new critique is an aggression against reactive forces and their philosophical embodiment, dialectics. Nietzsche sets up a new image of thought, which rejects the field of truth in favour of that of sense and value.[23]

It is difficult to know what to do with this account of Nietzsche. Deleuze does not link this view of philosophy as radical critique to any account of the status of that critique and its positive products. Despite the 'aggression against traditional philosophy', Deleuze's Nietzsche seems to be engaged in the most traditional of philosophical projects: the unmasking of illusion. The old philosophy is attacked as insufficiently critical, for not referring us to 'the *real* forces that form thought'[24] – as if the 'new thought' will be able to be 'more accurate'. Deleuze appears to ignore the reflexive self-awareness that is constitutive of Nietzsche's texts,[25] while he uses the philosphical ruins it leaves behind to reconstruct, in Nietzsche's name, an old-fashioned philosophical system.

Richard Rorty seems fully justified in describing *Nietzsche and Philosophy* as a work that takes seriously 'the metaphysical system-building side of Nietzsche'.[26] It cannot be disputed that Deleuze sets out a 'Nietzschean system'. The question is: to what extent can it be described as 'metaphysical' or 'serious'? There is little doubt that, if it is a 'serious metaphysical system', it is not a 'respectable' one. According to Rorty, it uses 'flexible definitions' that make it possible to 'say practically anything one likes and make it sound harshly inevitable'.[27] As a result, he says, 'Deleuze dissolves everything into a mush of reactive forces in order to bring out their underlying nastiness.'[28] Rorty does not object to what he calls 'the good work of dialectical subversion' (what Deleuze calls 'critical aggression') but to the 'neologistic system building *ex nihilo*'.[29] Deleuze is accused of having cut 'all argumentative links' with common sense and the philosophical tradition.[30] This last objection is strangely reminiscent of attacks on Rorty's own work: cut yourself off from 'truth as correspondence to reality' and all 'cognitive controls' are lost. But Rorty's point is a different one. He does not object to the Deleuzean-Nietzschean attack on 'truth' and 'reality'; to the fact that the enterprise is not 'controlled' by reference to reality; rather, he objects to the fact that there is an enterprise at all. It is not that Deleuze goes too far but that he does not go far enough. In Rorty's view, when the 'good work of dialectical subversion' has been properly carried through, all that can remain is the continuation of the conversation of our culture, 'edifying philosophy'. The construction of philosophical systems is part of the misconceived attempt to provide 'foundations' for the traditions within which we think.

This brings us to the central question of philosophy after Nietzsche: is a 'positive philosophical enterprise' possible 'after reflexivity'? To see the force of this question we can again look at Deleuze's Nietzsche. Vincent Descombes puts forward a number of criticisms of Deleuze in his book *Modern French Philosophy*.[31] These are not directly reflexive in form but they once again direct attention to the status of the Nietzschean story as told by Deleuze. Descombes sees Deleuze trying to provide general criteria for differentiating between active and reactive, 'between that which originates from the Slave and that which originates from the Master'.[32] More generally, the question is 'how can *difference* be reintroduced into a world menaced by indifference without going back on the lesson of the Copernican revolution that "we are giving the orders"?'[33] This is the general dilemma of perspectivism. Once it is accepted that the organisation of the world is not an external given, how can we adopt a critical perspective? From what vantage point can we criticize? According to Descombes, Deleuze's key distinction is between 'difference' and 'opposition'. The Master begins from his own sovereign affirmation, the Slave from his negation of the Master. The Slave *opposes* the Master, but the Master *differs from* the Slave. Recognising that no criterion of differentiation can be *external* to all judging, Deleuze attempts to provide one that is *internal* to judging itself. The aporias of perspectivism are escaped by the self-validation of one particular perspective: that of the Master.

But, Descombes argues, this will not work. The internal criterion of judgment is manifestly inapplicable. From the perspective of the Master, negation is not negative but different, while from the perspective of the Slave, affirmation is an opposition.[34] There is no 'external', third perspective from which Master and Slave can be compared. Organisation has not been introduced into an indifferent world. Furthermore, the whole project is, in Deleuze's own terms, a doubtful one. Who but the

Slave would wish to have a general criterion for distinguishing Master from Slave? The very distinction between Master and Slave is a slavish one: such things are no concern of the Masters. The whole idea of a 'general semiology' and an 'ethics and ontology' seems to belong to the central tradition of Western metaphysics and, as such, to a Christian and reactive project. In attacking the 'thought of the Slave', Deleuze's Nietzsche seems, unwittingly, to have reproduced it.

The problem is not merely that Deleuze has produced a 'mushy' system but rather that to produce a system at all is to reproduce the thought of the Slave, to fall into the reflexive self-annihilation of nihilism. This can be seen from the notion of 'critique' which Deleuze uses to characterise Nietzsche's project. It is not simply that critique must be directed against 'truth' and 'knowledge' – it must also be directed against itself. For the notion of 'critique' lies at the heart of Western metaphysics: a critique is always in complicity with that which it criticises. As Lyotard says, the activity of critique

is profoundly rational, profoundly consistent with the system. Profoundly reformist: the critic remains in the sphere of the criticized, he belongs to it, he goes beyond one term of the position but doesn't alter the position of terms.[35]

Deleuze is accused of having restored Nietzsche to the freedom of the city of philosophy in order to confine him there, of having presented a conformist, reactive Nietzsche, imprisoned by his own concepts. How would Deleuze deal with such an accusation? How are such objections to be dealt with? They must be approached indirectly. As Deleuze once said, 'Every time someone makes an objection to me, I want to say, "Okay, okay, let's go on to something else. Objections have never contributed anything."'[36] The space of objections is the sedentary space of negation. We must not simply move back and forth within it – although, as we shall see, there is no simple 'escape' from it.

A first step on such an indirect approach to these reflexive criticisms is the later discussion of Nietzsche by Deleuze. This occurred at a 1972 conference which brought together many leading Nietzsche scholars and which can be seen as one result of Deleuze's own earlier book. In this very different strategic context Deleuze takes what appears to be a very different approach to

Nietzsche. He now stands not at the beginning of post-history but at the 'dawn of counterculture'.[37] Whilst Marx and Freud aim to recodify the state and the family, Nietzsche 'assists in the attempt at decodification . . . in an absolute sense, by expressing something that cannot be codified, confounding all codes'.[38] Nietzsche's aphorisms must be understood in terms of a 'deterritorialisation'. Philosophy is essentially related to the machinery of codification, it is part of the history of sedentary peoples. Nietzsche's position is very different:

> If Nietzsche does not belong to philosophy, it is perhaps because he was the first to conceive of another kind of discourse as counter-philosophy. This discourse is above all nomadic; its statements can be conceived as the products of a mobile war machine and not the utterances of rational administrative machinery whose philosophers would be bureaucrats of pure reason.[39]

Deleuze's Nietzsche is now not a 'philosopher of sense and values'. He is not a philosopher at all. Deleuze describes him in the terms provided by his own work with Felix Guattari in the 1970s, the so-called 'philosophy of desire'. Does this involve a fundamental change of approach? Both Descombes and Rorty claim that it does not. They see the change as mere word-play, a simple change in terminology, expressing the same basic views.[40] Deleuze's own riposte is simple: 'How pleasant it will be if people say: this time they've let us down, they've gone mad! And if they say: it's always the same old story with them, better still. We are elsewhere.'[41] But the account which Deleuze and Guattari give of this new terminology suggests a way of dealing with the 'reflexive objections' to the earlier account of Nietzsche.

In Deleuze and Guattari's work the old dualisms of active and reactive, affirmative and negative, Master and Slave no longer play a central part. They have been replaced by a whole series of new dualisms: nomadic and sedentary, deterritorialisation and reterritorialisation, decoding and recoding, molecular and molar, rhizome and tree, and so on. How do these function in the later texts? A common reaction is to say that all these dualisms are, in effect, the old dualism of 'good' and 'bad' under a series of weird and wonderful new names – the first term being good and the second bad. But none of these dualisms is used in such a straightforward way; rather they are woven into complex webs of interconnections.

A version of Deleuze and Guattari's 'method' is set out in *Rhizome*, the Introduction to *Thousand Plateaux*.[42] This account uses the dualism of rhizome and tree. The image of the tree has dominated the whole of Western thought; its roots are always referred back to the unity of the trunk. When roots divide they always divide in two. Thus, 'binary logic is the spiritual unity of the root tree'.[43] The rhizome, on the other hand, has no point of origin or aim. It has no central unifying principle, growing in all directions, and always 'growing from the middle'. A rhizome is heterogeneous, a multiplicity, it is flat; no idea of genetic axis or deep structure can be applied to it. It is a surface, a plateau on whose surface intensities are in a state of continuous variation. Each discussion, each set of operations with one or more dualism, forms a plateau – any point on the rhizome can be connected to any other point.

But, once again, the reflexive objection can be put: is not this rhizome-tree dualism and all the other dualisms that proliferate on their plateaux simply another version of the binary logic of the tree? Have Deleuze and Guattari not, once again, unwittingly reproduced, in the very act of attack, that which they are attacking? In the later work this objection is dealt with in two ways. First, each side of the dualism is so bound up with the other as to call any simple dualism into question for, 'tree or root structures exist in rhizomes, but the converse is also true; a tree branch or root section can begin to burgeon into rhizomes'.[44] Because 'there is no dualism, no ontological dualism or here and there, no axiological dualism of good and bad, no American style blend or synthesis. There are nodes of arborescence in rhizomes and rhizomatic shoots in roots.'[45] Apparently simple dualisms always break down under sustained development into a series of complex overlapping and interconnecting terms. Each dualism is twisted, bent, and made to do new work. As Deleuze says, 'We go as far as possible in developing radical oppositions.'[47] These descriptions of the multiple interrelations of apparently simple dualisms show that the straightforwardly Manichaean view of Deleuze and Guattari cannot be sustained. But this is, in itself, no answer to the reflexive objection. These accounts can, once again, be turned back upon themselves and subjected to an apparently remorseless 'binary logic': either they are 'ordered representations' of some pre-existent reality, in which case they are aborescent attempts to re-territorialise desires, or they are not, in which case they appear to be simple fictions of no 'theoretical' interest.

This brings us back to the central question of philosophy after Nietzsche: is a positive philosophical enterprise possible after re-flexivity? Deleuze and Guattari do not, contrary to first impressions, simply ignore this question. The few comments they make about the status of their own enterprise indicate a reply that appears surprisingly close to that of Jacques Derrida. Like Derrida's radically undecidable, Janus-faced, 'non-concepts', Deleuze and Guattari's dualisms and the descriptions that employ them have an explicit *strategic* function:

> We invoke one dualism only in order to challenge another. We employ a dualism of models only in order to arrive at a process which would challenge all models. It is up to the reader to have cerebral correctors which undo the dualisms that we have not wished to draw, but by which nevertheless we travel. It is up to the reader to arrive at the magic formula which we all seek: PLURALISM = MONISM, by passing through all the dualisms which are the enemy, the altogether necessary enemy, the furniture which we endlessly shift around.[48]

Dualisms cannot be abolished but they can be used strategically, to challenge other dualisms and to push in a certain direction, a direction that can – to use a phrase familiar to analytical philosophers – only be shown, not said.

Thus, Deleuze and Guattari do, in this way, directly confront the problem of reflexivity. The question of the status of their own work is raised and turns out to be built into its very structure. Any dualism encompasses, in a certain way, all the others. This allows them to describe their method as 'rhizomatic' – the rhizome-tree dualism apparently being set up as primary. Elsewhere, however, as in the 1972 discussion of Nietzsche, the decoding-recoding dualism appears to be the central one. Yet again, the most fundamental dualism seems to be that between the nomadic and the sedentary. These examples could be multiplied. This does not show that Deleuze and Guattari are simply confused and contradictory, but that their wildly poliferating dualisms are arranged in such a way that none can take final precedence, that each undoes all the others in its different developments.

In summary, therefore, Deleuze and Guattari's 'theories' do not claim to be 'true' or 'accurate' representations of 'reality'. Nor do they claim 'scientificity', for they 'no more recognise scientificity than . . . ideology'.[49] Instead, the aim of all these strange constructions is strategic: to push us in a certain direction, to connect up certain multiplicities until we catch on – or not, as the case may be.[50] The Deleuzean strategist aims to construct assemblages (*agencements*) that will connect up multiple elements, that will work in different ways. Every assemblage is always misleading always on its way to becoming fixed and 'recoded', to losing its force. Every assemblage also, in a certain way, exemplifies the overall strategy. As Deleuze says, 'to shout "long live the multiple" is not to make it, we must make the multiple'.[51] All Deleuze's 'systems' can be regarded as temporary strategic constructions, as the transitory fortifications of an advancing nomadic war machine. They are, to use Lyotard's term, 'stories' or 'accounts' (*récits*).[52] The different parts of the narrative are woven into the storyline in different ways. Their relations are not 'logical' ones, although there are narrative consistencies and narrative entailments. Such narratives are not to be simply judged or analysed but to be used. As Deleuze says, 'concepts are exactly like sounds, colours or images, they are intensities which either suit you or don't, which are accepted or aren't accepted'.[53] Narratives cannot be 'refuted' or 'disproved' – if they are not accepted or do not work we pass on to something else. No narrative can take definitive precedence over any other – although different narratives can take precedence in different situations. A narrative is still a theory in the sense that it advances an 'explanation', but an explanation that can never claim to be final or definitive, an explanation that works by redescribing events so that they fit into a particular story put together for a particular practical purpose in a particular situation. So, according to Deleuze, 'A theory is exactly like a box of tools. It has nothing to do with the signifier. It must be useful. It must function. And not for itself.'[54] Practice does not provide a criterion of truth but particular criteria are constructed to respond to particular practical situations. There is a new relationship between theory and practice. 'The relationships between theory and practice . . . are partial and fragmentary. . . . Practice is a set of relays from one theoretical point to another, and theory is a relay from one practice to another.'[55] A narrative is a theory that does not claim general application. 'A theory does not totalise; it is multiplied, it multiplies.'[56] Thus, according to Deleuze, there 'is no general recipe. We have finished with all globalising concepts. Even concepts are . . . events.'[57]

And now I hestitate . . . I have been seeking to give you the narrative of all narratives. I have pretended to occupy a non-existent place – 'outside' all the proliferating narratives I have pretended to describe. Reflexivity allows no escape of this kind. The only way out is to ignore it – and that in a certain way. By such ignoring it is hoped that you – and I – will catch on and perhaps arrive at the magic formula which the philosophers, from Nagarjuna to Deleuze, have been seeking.[58]

Yet now, perhaps, something more can be said about the way in which Deleuze 'takes seriously' the systematic side of of Nietzsche. For Deleuze, a 'system' is an invention, an assemblage constructed from heterogeneous elements – elements that, in this case, are drawn from Nietzsche's texts. The aim is not textual fidelity, but the construction of an assemblage – an assemblage which combines with 'extra-textual practice' in productive ways. As Deleuze said in a discussion of his 1972 Nietzsche paper, 'For me a text is only a little wheel in an extra-textual practice. . . . It's a matter of seeing what use a text is in the extra-textual practice which draws out the text.'[59] Deleuze constructs an assemblage with Nietzschean materials. This assemblage is taken seriously, yet with a seriousness that belongs not to the 'spirit of gravity' but to humour, for 'one cannot help but laugh when the codes are confounded'.[60] It is seriousness that emerges after the spirit of gravity is dispersed in a gale of Dionysian laughter.

Far from being, in Rorty's phrase, overcome by nostalgia for the 'Grand Hotel Abgrund',[61] Deleuze is rejecting all ideas of abyssal ground or origin in favour of an undelimited proliferation of narratives. In contrast to Rorty's passive pragmatism, which has 'no more to offer than common sense . . . about knowledge and truth',[62] Deleuze is advancing, or rather practising, a constructive pragmatism. He begins where Rorty leaves off. The aim is not the urbane continuation of cultural conversation, but the exhilarating and dangerous task of post-modernity, 'the manufacture of materials to harness forces, to think the unthinkable'.[63] This does not involve a straightforward 'going beyond' philosophy. On the one hand, it is philosophy in the traditional sense.[64] On the other, it is something entirely different, an affirmative counter-philosophy, Platonism routed. It is between the two that Deleuze operates: the rhizome always grows from the middle. The 1962 book was called *Nietzsche* and *Philosophy*, 'the AND gives relations another direction and puts to flight both terms and wholes, on the line of flight which it actively creates'.[65]

The model city of philosophy is under constant threat from the nomadic war machine, but the nomads never try to sack the city. Instead, its inhabitants constantly find themselves caught up in treacherous plots against the authorities. Deleuze has restored Nietzsche to that dangerous group of impostors, the counter-thinkers who are neither philosophers nor non-philosophers. They are 'the ones who do *not* move and begin to nomadise in order to stay in the same place while escaping the codes'.[66] Excitement always happens on the edge of town.

Notes

1 Gilles Deleuze, *Nietzsche and Philosophy*, translated Hugh Tomlinson, London; The Athlone Press, 1983 (henceforth *NP*)

2 Sarah Kofman, *Nietzsche et la scène philosophique*, Paris: Union Generale d'Editions, 1979, p.7

3 Paul de Man, 'Action and Identity in Nietzsche', *Yale French Studies*, No.52, 1975, p.16

4 See, for example, Walter Kaufmann, *Nietzsche: Philosopher, Psychologist, Antichrist*, Princeton; Princeton University Press, 1950, 4th Edn 1974; Richard Schacht, *Nietzsche*, London, Routledge & Kegan Paul, 1983

5 See Jacques Derrida, *Spurs: Nietzsche's Styles*, translated Barbara Harlow, Chicago: University of Chicago Press, 1979; Paul de Man, *Allegories of Reading: figural language in Rousseau, Nietzsche, Rilke and Proust*, New Haven; Yale University Press, 1979; and see also Hilary Lawson, *Reflexivity: the post-modern predicament*, London, Hutchinson, 1985 and Alexander Nehamas, *Nietzsche: Life as Literature*, Cambridge, Mass., Harvard University Press, 1985.

6 *NP*, p.1

7 *NP*, p.62

8 Gilles Deleuze, *Nietzsche*, Paris; Presses Universitaires de France 1965, (henceforth, *N*), pp.24–25

9 *NP* p.54

10 *N* p.25

11 loc.cit.
12 *NP* p.119
13 *NP* p.x
14 *NP* p.139
15 *NP* pp.70–71 and pp.174–175
16 *NP* p.70
17 *NP* p.86
18 *NP* p.106
19 loc.cit.
20 *NP* p.88
21 *NP* p.89
22 *NP* p.94
23 *NP* p.104
24 *NP* p.103 (my emphasis)
25 See Lawson, op.cit., Chapter 2
26 Richard Rorty, 'Unsoundness in Perspective', *Times Literary Supplement*, June 17, 1983, p.619
27 Ibid., p.620
28 Ibid., p.619
29 Ibid., p.620
30 loc.cit.
31 Cambridge, Cambridge University Press, 1980
32 Ibid., p.159
33 Ibid., p.166
34 Ibid., pp.164–165
35 Jean-Francois Lyotard, *Dérive à partir de Marx et Freud*, Paris, Union Generale d'Editions, 1973, p.14; *Driftworks*, New York, Semiotext(e), 1984, 13 (translation modified)
36 Gilles Deleuze and Claire Parnet, *Dialogues*, Paris; Flammarion, 1977, p.7 (henceforth *D*); *Dialogues*, translated Hugh Tomlinson and Barbara Habberjam, London, The Athlone Press, 1987
37 Gilles Deleuze, 'Pensée Nomade', in *Nietzsche Aujourd'Hui?*, Tome 1, Paris; Union Generale d'Editions, 1973; 'Nomad Thought', in *The New Nietzsche*, edited David B. Allison, New York, Delta, 1977 (henceforth *NT*), p.142
38 *NT* p.143
39 *NT* p.149
40 Descombes, op.cit, pp.174–175; Rorty, op.cit, p.619
41 Gilles Deleuze and Felix Guattari, *Rhizome: Introduction*, Paris Minuit, 1976; 'Rhizome', in *I & C*, No.8, Spring 1981, (henceforth *R*), p.67. A slightly different version of this text can be found as the Introduction to Gilles Deleuze and Felix Guattari, *Mille Plateaux*, Paris, Minuit, 1980; *Thousand Plateaux*, translated Brian Massumi, London, The Athlone Press, forthcoming.
42 see note 41

43 *R* p.51
44 *R* p.60
45 *R* p.63
46 See *The Anti-Oedipus*, translated R. Hurley, M. Seem, and H.R. Lane, London, The Athlone Press, 1985
47 Gilles Deleuze, Vincennes Seminar, 6 December 1977
48 *R* p.64 (translation modified)
49 *R* p.65
50 See, generally, The Second of January Group, *After Truth: a postmodern manifesto*, London, Inventions Press, 1986
51 *D* p.23
52 See, generally, Jean-Francois Lyotard, *The Postmodern Condition: A Report on Knowledge*, translated Geoff Bennington and Brian Massumi, Manchester, Manchester University Press, 1986
53 *D* p.10
54 'Intellectuals and Power: a conversation between Michel Foucault and Gilles Deleuze', in Michel Foucault, *Language, Counter-Memory, Practice*, ed. D.F. Bouchard, Oxford, Basil Blackwell, p.208
55 Ibid., pp.205–206
56 Ibid., p.208 (translation modifed)
57 *D* p.173
58 See Second of January Group, op.cit, pp.21–31
59 *Nietzsche aujourd'hui?*, Vol 1, (see note 37), p.186
60 *NT* p.147; see also *D* p.83
61 Rorty, op.cit., p.620
62 Richard Rorty, *Philosophy and the Mirror of Nature*, Oxford, Basil Blackwell, 1980, p.176
63 Gilles Deleuze, Vincennes Seminar, 7 March 1978
64 *L'Arc*, No.49, Second Edition, 1980, p.99
65 *D* p.71
66 *NT* p.149

· 10 ·

Nietzsche
and the Critique of
Ursprungsphilosophie

PETER DEWS

In a celebrated section of *Götzen-Dämmerung*, Nietzsche describes what he takes to have been the role of 'reason' in philosophy. Reaffirming an advocacy of 'historical philosophizing' (*historisches Philosophieren*) which has been central to his work ever since the opening paragraphs of *Human, All-too-Human*, he suggests that one of the most dangerous idiosyncrasies of philosophers has been 'to confuse the first and the last':

> They place that which comes at the end – unfortunately! for it ought not to come at all! – namely, the 'highest concepts', which means the most general, the emptiest concepts, the last smoke of an evaporating reality, in the beginning, as the beginning. This again is nothing but their way of showing reverence: the higher may not grow out of the lower, may not have grown at all . . . That which is last, thinnest and emptiest is put first as cause in itself, as *ens realissimum*.[1]

For Nietzsche, the role allotted to the I or ego (*das Ich*) in modern thought is the most obvious embodiment of this inversion. The ego recommends itself for such a role, because of our apparently immediate awareness of the contents of consciousness: 'To derive something unknown from something known alleviates, calms, gratifies and furthermore gives a feeling of power.'[2] Yet this immediacy of self-knowledge is, for Nietzsche, an illusion, and consequently so are the unity and identity which the ego projects into things:

Formerly, alteration, change, any becoming at all, were taken as proof of mere appearance, as an indication that there must be something which led us astray. Today, conversely, precisely in so far as the prejudice of reason forces us to posit unity, identity, permanence, substance, cause, thinghood, being, we see ourselves caught in error, compelled into error.[3]

Nietzsche's arguments against the 'philosophy of origins', and his connection of such philosophy with the coercive imposition of an identity whose model is that of the self-conscious subject, have had an important impact on contemporary intellectual life, particularly through the mediation of recent French thought. Yet Nietzsche's position is clearly not unproblematic. For the undermining of original identity, and consequently of any comprehensive conceptualization of reality, seems to depend – either surreptitiously or explicitly – on an ontology of flux which is incompatible with the critical motifs in Nietzsche's own thought. Thus, in the section of *Götzen-Dämmerung* which we have been considering, Nietzsche suggests that even Heraclitus did injustice to the senses in so far as he considered them to be the purveyors of an illusion of stability and identity.[4] Yet it can scarcely be denied that our experience of the empirical world is characterised both by (relative) change *and* (relative) identity. It is not clear in what sense Nietzsche can appeal to an absolute priority of becoming, or insist upon the *inherently* falsifying and fetishizing function of concepts.

These difficulties are no less prominent in the work of those recent French thinkers who have been influenced by Nietzsche, as can be seen from Foucault's essay on 'Nietzsche, Genealogy, History'.[5] Here Foucault seeks to give a condensed exposition of Nietzsche's critique of *Ursprungsphilosophie*, and to delineate his genealogical alternative. According to Foucault, Nietzsche frequently employs the concept of 'origin' (*Ursprung*) in a stressed opposition to those of 'descent' (*Herkunft*) and 'emergence' (*Entstehung*). The origin is the traditional goal of philosophers; the pursuit of the origin consists in 'an attempt to capture the exact essence of things, their purest possibilities, and their carefully protected identities . . . ; this search assumes the existence of immobile forms that precede the external world of accident and succession.'[6] *Entstehung* and *Herkunft*, by contrast, form the object not of a philosophical quest but of a new kind of history. The question of 'descent' is the question of the transmission and intermingling of racial and social characteristics, and of the body as the 'inscribed surface of events',[7] while 'emergence' must be understood in terms of the 'non-place' of opposition between forces which deprives the phenomenon of any single source.[8] Thus, Nietzschean genealogy, in its concern for *Herkunft* and *Entstehung*, shatters the identity of the subject and erases the uniqueness of the source. Genealogy, Foucault suggests, is opposed to 'the search for "origins"' and to 'the meta-historical deployment of ideal significations'.[9]

Throughout this text, Foucault opposes the conflictuality, singularity and dispersion of the real events of history described by genealogy to the 'profound intentions and immutable necessities' of *Ursprungphilosophie*. Yet in describing the standpoint of genealogy he finds himself entangled in a contradiction that is similar to the one we have already encountered in Nietzsche. For, on the one hand, he argues that the aim of genealogy is to 'leave things undisturbed in their own dimension and intensity',[10] to respect the actual complexity and diversity of events. On the other hand, he argues that genealogy is directed against the ideal of 'apocalyptic objectivity': Nietzsche's version of historical sense

is explicit in its perspective and acknowledges its system of injustice. . . . It is not given to a discreet effacement before the objects it observes and does not submit itself to their processes; nor does it seek laws, since it gives equal weight to its own sight and to its objects.[11]

Foucault does not attempt to reconcile these two accounts: genealogy is presented as being both 'gray, meticulous and patiently documentary',[12] and as being marked – like all interpretations – by an element of the coercive and the arbitrary.

The extent to which 'Nietzsche, Genealogy, History' can be read as a methodological manifesto for Foucault's work of the 1970s, rather than simply as an exposition of Nietzsche, is open to debate. However, even setting this question aside, it is clear that difficulties similar to those which emerge in that essay have characterised Foucault's thought ever since the beginning. Thus in his most explicit phase of methodological reflection, around the time of *The Archaeology of Knowledge*, Foucault describes himself as being committed to a 'pure description of the facts of discourse', despite the fact that his own theory of discursive formations is explicitly directed against any phenomenological

conception of pure description.[13] The conclusion to *The Archaeology of Knowledge* is one of the few places in Foucault's work
where this tension between objectivism and relativism is explicitly
reflected upon. Here Foucault admits that the attempt to bypass
any enquiry into the conditions of possibility of knowledge runs
the risk of accusations of naïveté; he therefore tries – without
notable success – to define a status for his historical description of
discursive formations which would be neither that of science nor
of philosophy.[14] Ultimately, however, Foucault's sympathies lie
with the scientific challenge to philosophical perspectives: 'if you
recognize the right of empirical research, some fragment of
history, to challenge the transcendental dimension, then you have
ceded the main point'.[15]

In similar forms, the difficulties which we have outlined in
Foucault occur also in the other French thinkers of the 1960s and
1970s most directly influenced by Nietzsche. In Jean-François
Lyotard's *Économie libidinale*, the autonomy and priority of the
concept and of consciousness is challenged from the standpoint of
an ontology of force. However, the impossibility of justifying this
ontology theoretically then leads to an aestheticization of
philosophical discourse. But this aestheticization in turn requires
some form of justification, and when the political consequences in
terms of which the suspension of truth-claims was legitimated turn
out not to be those which were anticipated, then the entire
structure begins to collapse. By the time of *Just Gaming* (1979),
Lyotard has renounced his metaphysics of libido, and has
admitted that 'it is not true that the quest for intensities or things
of that kind can provide the substance of a politics, because there
is the problem of injustice'.[16]

There is one thinker within the field of post-structuralism,
however, whose work does not fall victim to these difficulties.
Although Jacques Derrida has been deeply influenced by Nietzsche,
his primary training as a philosopher was within the tradition of
Husserlian phenomenology, and as a consequence he has always
retained a sense of the integrity of the transcendental perspective,
and of its invulnerability to direct historicist or naturalistic
inversions. One obvious testimony to this difference of outlook is
Derrida's review of Foucault's *Madness and Civilization*, which
challenges the coherence of Foucault's conception of an empirical
history of reason. For Derrida, 'the internal and autonomous

analysis of the philosophical content of philosophical discourse' must take priority over any historical insertion.[17] We cannot write the history of reason until we know what reason is – and history alone can never tell us this, since in any historical investigation reason is presupposed. In consequence, Derrida concludes – with deliberate provocation – that the 'reduction to intraworldliness' of the hyperbolic *cogito* is itself potentially a form of totalitarian enclosure no less dangerous than those which Foucault attacks.[18]

It should be noted that Derrida's objections are not aimed simply against direct attempts to invert the relation of priority between the essential and the factual. More generally, Derrida is opposed to any philosophical strategy intended to blur or weaken the line between the empirical and the transcendental realms. This opposition is clearly exemplified in Derrida's earliest major essay, his 'Introduction' to Husserl's posthumously published text on 'The Origin of Geometry' – an exploration of the problem of origins which had also intrigued Merleau-Ponty. Interestingly, Merleau-Ponty reads this late meditation by Husserl as one symptom of a shift away from *Ursprungsphilosophie*, as Nietzsche understands it: genetic phenomenology can be seen as an attempt not to place the ideal and immutable at the origin, but rather precisely to see how idealities – such as those of geometry – emerge out of the flux and instability of the life world.[19] More generally, Merleau-Ponty perceives in Husserl's later work a renunciation of the view that transcendental reflection can function independently of all empirical investigation. He suggests that the later Husserl

seems to admit that the philosopher could not possibly have immediate access to the universal by reflection alone – that he is in no position to do without anthropological experience or to construct what constitutes the meaning of other experiences and civilizations by a purely imaginative variation of his own experiences.[20]

Merleau-Ponty is not, of course, advocating the elimination of the transcendental perspective. But he is challenging its self-sufficiency, and suggesting that such a challenge emerges by virtue of the internal dynamic of Husserl's phenomenology itself.

However, in his 'Introduction' to 'The Origin of Geometry', Derrida is explicitly hostile to this softening of the distinction between transcendental and empirical enquiry. For Derrida, to admit that empirical facts could have any status other than that of examples for the procedure of imaginative variation 'contradicts the very premiss of phenomenology', which is that 'essential insight *de jure* precedes every material historical investigation, and has no need of facts as such to reveal to the historian the a priori sense of his activity and objects'.[21] In general, Derrida opposes Merleau-Ponty's thesis of a *historicization* of phenomenology, which argues that, to the very extent that Husserl in his later work makes history an explicit object of enquiry, his phenomenology is able to liberate itself from history, rather than being unwittingly subject to it. Derrida writes: 'We could then be tempted by an interpretation diametrically opposed to that of Merleau-Ponty, and maintain that Husserl, far from opening the phenomenological parentheses to historical factuality under all its forms, leaves history more than ever *outside* them.'[22]

Derrida's resistance to the dilution of the transcendental perspective cannot help but raise questions about his own attitude to the philosophy of origins. For, if Derrida defends the primacy of transcendental enquiry, he must surely also be committed to the derivative status of the empirical. And yet one of the most prominent and influential of Derrida's themes has been the criticism of all philosophical conceptions of origin. It is precisely the absence of origin – or of a *telos*, its mirror-image or counterpart – which blocks the possibility of interpretive closure and opens up the dissemination of the text. Thus Derrida's strategy must take the form of an internal dismantling of the transcendental perspective, which prevents it from performing its founding or originating role, without lapsing into what he would consider to be the incoherence of a prioritization, or even equalization, of empirical enquiry.

In order to clarify what is at stake here, it may be useful to refer to an earlier episode in the history of philosophy, in which the status of transcendental philosophy was similarly at issue: the clash between Fichte and Schelling, perhaps *the* crucial episode in the development of German Idealism. The parallel suggests itself, because the difficulties which Schelling confronted in his attempt to move beyond what he considered to be Fichte's subjective idealism are close to those which Derrida confronts in his effort to transcend the phenomenology of Husserl. In both cases what is confronted is a conception of philosophy as 'systematic self-investigation'[23] as the reflexive explication of the structure of consciousness. In· Husserl, it is true, this explication is eidetic and descriptive, whereas in Fichte it is dialectical-deductive. Yet what is common to both is the conviction that a standpoint has been attained which cannot be gone beyond: there can be no other knowledge more fundamental than self-knowledge, since in all other knowledge the self is presupposed. Thus, in the 1794 *Wissenschaftslehre*, Fichte opposes 'the concept of an existent that is supposed, from a certain viewpoint, to subsist independently of presentation' on the grounds that 'whatever we may think, we are that which thinks therein, and hence . . . nothing could ever come to exist independently of us, for everything is necessarily related to our thinking'.[24] Similarly, in the *Cartesian Meditations*, Husserl argues that

> Every imaginable sense, every imaginable being, whether the latter is called immanent or transcendent, falls within the domain of transcendental subjectivity, as the subjectivity which constitutes sense and being. The attempt to conceive the universe of true being as something lying outside the universe of possible consciousness, possible knowledge, possible evidence, the two being related to one another merely externally by a rigid law, is nonsensical.[25]

Such positions appear, at first sight, to be impregnable. Yet, in his divergence from Fichte, Schelling focuses on one crucial weakness. Transcendental idealism claims to have found an absolute starting point, yet any self-consciousness contains a duality of subject and object, even though the object here is merely the subject reflected upon by itself. Yet every object is conditioned by its relation to a subject, just as every subject is conditioned by its relation to an object, so that neither taken alone, nor the two their relation, can constitute the absolute standpoint that is claimed. Schelling had already developed this argument clearly in his early (1795) essay, 'Vom Ich als Princip der Philosophie Überhaupt':

> Since the subject is thinkable only in regard to an object, and the object only in regard to a subject, neither of them can contain the unconditional because both are conditioned reciprocally, both are equally unserviceable. Furthermore, in order to determine the relationship of the two, an ulterior reason for the determination must be presupposed, owing to which both

are determined. For one cannot say that the subject alone determines the object, because the subject is only conceivable in relation to the object, and vice versa, and it would amount to the same if I were to treat as unconditional a subject determined by an object or an object determined by a subject.[26]

In this essay, Schelling resolves the difficulty by distinguishing between the subject and what he terms the 'absolute I', which is beyond the subject-object relation. Eventually, however, he comes to appreciate that what is beyond this relation can be characterized neither in objective nor in subjective terms, but is rather in a state of 'absolute indifference' (*absolute Indifferenz*) with regard to all determinations. From the new standpoint of Schelling's *Identitätsphilosophie*, Fichte's insistence on the primacy of the evidence of reflection, his assertion that 'one cannot begin from a being . . . but must begin from a seeing'[27] simply confirms the limitations of his philosophy, since the metaphor of vision implies the duality of viewer and viewed. In his reply to Fichte, Schelling argues that 'The necessity of beginning from seeing keeps you and your philosophy locked within a thoroughly conditioned sequence.'[28] He points out that

Either you must never move outside seeing, as you express it, and this means outside subjectivity, and *every I*, as you say at one point in the *Wissenschaftslehre*, must be and remain the absolute substance, or, if you go out to an unconceptualizable real ground, then the whole reference back to subjectivity is only valid in a preliminary sense.[29]

It is difficult to overlook the parallels between Schelling's arguent and Derrida's critique of Husserl. Derrida, as we have seen, resists any externalist reduction – or even qualification – of transcendental consciousness. Rather, he focuses on the discrepancy between the claim of the immediacy of the relation of phenomenological self-presence, and the necessarily conditioned nature of any such relation. Like Schelling, Derrida insists on the derivative status of, and attempts to climb beyond, the classical oppositions of philosophy: 'Subjectivity – like objectivity – is an effect of *différance*, an effect inscribed in a system of *différance*.'[30] It could be replied, of course, that such a comparison is superficial. Schelling transcends the subject-object relation towards absolute identity, a point of ultimate closure and security, whereas Derrida's *différance* implies perpetual deferral of any such point.

Yet even this objection is not as convincing as may at first appear. Firstly, because a *différance* which is prior to all determinate differences collapses into absolute identity: as François Wahl noted long ago, 'a bare concept of *différance* is a contradiction, since difference has to be specified'.[31] And secondly, because it follows from Schelling's argument that the absolute cannot become an object of consciousness, cannot be made present any more than *différance*. It is therefore not surprising that Schelling's thought – like that of Derrida – is accompanied by an incessant reflection on its own conditions of meaningfulness. The restless character of the work of both Derrida and Schelling can be seen not as a manifestation of inconsistency, but rather as a logical consequence of their point of departure: it is only through the repeated development, and the repeated collapse, of philosophical terminologies and strategies that something of the nature of philosophy's 'impossible' object can be obliquely indicated.[32]

If there is any plausibility in this parallel between Derrida and Schelling, then the status of Derrida's attack on the concept of origin clearly needs to be reassessed. Derrida shows the impossibility of an origin, in the sense of an epistemological ground which could be made present. But he cannot be said to have abandoned the concept of origin, if we understand by 'origin' the unconditioned source of the conditioned structures of experience. This distinction is drawn by Derrida himslf in many of his statements concerning *différance* and the trace. Thus, in *Of Grammatology*, Derrida writes: 'There cannot be a science of differance itself in its operation, as it is impossible to have a science of the origin of presence itself, that is to say of a certain nonorigin.'[33] And a little later in the same chapter he remarks:

The trace is in fact the absolute origin of sense in general. Which amounts to saying once again that there is no absolute origin of sense in general. The trace is the differance which opens appearance and signification. Articulating the living upon the non-living in general, origin of all repetition, origin of ideality, the trace is not more ideal than real, not more intelligible than sensible, not more a transparent signification than an opaque energy, and no concept of metaphysics can describe it.[34]

Derrida himself has elsewhere stressed that 'neither/nor' is simultaneously 'either/or'[35], so that, in the light of such passages, it is difficult to deny the proximity of Derrida's *différance* to Schelling's *absolute Indifferenz*.

It seems that Derrida has avoided the contradictions of a reductive critique of *Ursprungsphilosophie* at the cost of reinstating the position which the critique was directed against. Nothing could be 'thinner' and 'emptier', to employ Nietzsche's terms, than the *différance* which Derrida makes responsible, not simply for the semantic instability of the text, but for the movement of the world and of history in general. The defence which is frequently made of Derrida at this point, that he is engaged in some form of parody of the philosophy of origins, is scarcely adequate. For if Derrida did not become involved in a certain argumentative strategy against transcendental philosophy, he would have no need of concepts of parody and of the *sous rature* in order to ward off the implications of his own position. The inherent difficulties of this strategy were perceptively pinpointed at an early date by Christopher Macann, in an article whose phenomenological standpoint produces an intriguing convergence with Nietzsche: 'Does Derrida's concept of "trace" or "*différance*" represent a transcendental critique of Husserl's transcendental analysis?' It may seem so at first.

And yet this return to an original principle, unlike Husserl's descriptions of the *Umwelt* or the *Lebenswelt*, seems to take us away from concrete structures of experience and to involve us in abstractions more abstruse than those of Husserl's transcendental analysis. Is the concept of the trace arrived at by a kind of reduction of the transcendental reduction to one single constitutive principle? But then, how can a principle attained exclusively through philosophical reflection be ascribed to consciousness as the condition of its realization?[36]

In fact, this is precisely the response which Fichte makes to Schelling when he suggests that the latter's absolute identity is purely negative and formal.[37]

Having reached this point, it seems legitimate to ask whether there is any sense in which Nietzsche's critique of *Ursprungsphilosophie* can be retained as a strength of contemporary thought, given the difficulties of both an externalist reduction of the standpoint of consciousness, and of Derrida's attempts to transcend that standpoint. I would argue that a positive answer to this question can be found in the work of Adorno, a thinker who plays off Nietzsche's insights against those of the dialectical tradition, in particular in his critique of Husserl's phenomenology – *Zur Metakritik der Erkenntnistheorie.*[38]

The significance of Adorno's position can perhaps best be brought out through a contrast with Derrida's assumption that the oppositions of metaphysics have always been thought within the horizon of their own overcoming; the duality of signifier and signified, for example, within the horizon of an ultimate unmediated presence of meaning. Derrida draws the following conclusion: 'The *paradox* is that the metaphysical reduction of the sign needed the opposition it was reducing. The opposition is systematic with the reduction.'[39] Yet, the second statement by no means follows from the first, unless one confuses a *historical* with an *essential* relation. For it could equally well be argued that duality has posed the most persistent problem and the most persistent block to projects of 'metaphysical reduction'. It is in this sense that Adorno appropriates the Nietzschean emphasis on the non-originality of conceptuality and consciousness:

The qualification of the absolutely first in subjective immanence founders because immanence can never completely disentangle the moment of non-identity within itself, and because subjectivity, the organ of reflection, clashes with the idea of an absolutely first as pure immediacy.[40]

Adorno should not be taken to mean, of course, that subjectivity as currently experienced and philosophically construed provides a barrier against the delusion of origins. Rather, his argument is that the suppression of non-identity, the collapsing of subjectivity into pure self-presence, against which Derrida protests, and the compulsive features of this suppression, which other post-structuralist thinkers have highlighted, are the expression of a historically and socially determined drive for control. It is for this reason that it is insufficient to oppose to identitarian principles an 'abstract asservation of polarity'.[41] Against even the reduction of duality, Adorno takes up the lesson of Nietzsche's thought that the philosophy of origins can only be dissolved, and the non self-sufficiency of the subject acknowledged, in the open-ended dialectic of concrete experience. Yet he moves beyond both Nietzsche and his more recent French followers in suggesting that the general possibility of such experience is a political question: the question of the practical overcoming of a redundant domination.

Notes

1 *GD*, 'Reason in Philosophy', para. 4
2 *GD*, 'The Four Great Errors', para. 5
3 *GD*, 'Reason in Philosophy', para. 5
4 *GD*, 'Reason in Philosophy', para. 2
5 Michel Foucault, 'Nietzsche, Genealogy, History', in Donald F. Bouchard, ed., *Language, Counter-Memory, Practice*, Oxford, Blackwell, 1977, pp.139–164
6 Ibid., p.142
7 Ibid., p.148
8 Ibid., p.150
9 Ibid., p.140
10 Ibid., p.154
11 Ibid., p.157
12 Ibid., p.139
13 See Michel Foucault, 'Réponse au Cercle d'épistemologie', in *Cahiers pour l'Analyse*, 9, Summer 1968, pp.9–40
14 See Michel Foucault, *The Archaeology of Knowledge*, London, Tavistock, 1972, pp.205–208
15 Ibid., p.203
16 Jean-François Lyotard and Jean-Loup Thébaud, *Au Juste*, Paris, Christian Bourgois, 1979, pp.170–171
17 Jacques Derrida, 'Cogito and the History of Madness', in *Writing and Difference*, London, Routledge & Kegan Paul, 1978, p.44
18 Ibid., p.57
19 For Merleau-Ponty's interpretation of the later Husserl, see 'La Philosophe et son Ombre', in *Éloge de la Philosophie*, Paris, Gallimard, 1960, pp.241–287
20 Maurice Merleau-Ponty, 'The Philosopher and Sociology', in John O'Neill, ed., *Phenomenology, Language and Sociology*, London, Heineman Educational, 1974, p.104
21 Jacques Derrida, *Edmund Husserl's Origin of Geometry: An Introduction*, Stony Brook, New York, Harvester, 1978, p.112
22 Ibid., p.116
23 Edmund Husserl, *Cartesian Meditations*, The Hague, Martinus Nijhoff, 1973, p.83
24 J.G. Fichte, 'Second Introduction to the Science of Knowledge', in Peter Heath and John Lachs, eds, *The Science of Knowledge*, Cambridge, Cambridge University of Press, 1982, p.71
25 *Cartesian Meditations*, p.84
26 F.W.J. Schelling, 'Of the I as Principle of Philosophy', in Fritz Marti trans. and ed., *The Unconditional in Human Knowledge*, New Jersey, Cranbury, 1980, p.74
27 J.G. Fichte, Letter to Schelling, 31 May–7 August 1801, in Walter

Schulz, ed., *Fichte-Schelling: Briefwechsel*, Frankfurt, 1968, p.126

28 F.W.J. Schelling, Letter to Fichte, 3 October 1801, in *Briefwechsel*, p.135

29 Ibid., p.134

30 Jacques Derrida, *Positions*, trans. Alan Bass, London, Athlone, 1981, p.28

31 'Un concept nu de différance est contradiction, car la différence ne peut manquer d'être spécifiée: *Qu'est-ce que le Structuralisme: Philosophie*, Paris, 1973, p.186

32 On this aspect of Schelling's thought, see Wolfgang Wieland, 'Die Anfänge der Philosophie Schellings und die Frage nach der Natur', in Manfred Frank and Gerhard Kurz, eds, *Materialien zu Schellings Philosophischen Anfängen*, Frankfurt, 1975, pp.250–254

33 Jacques Derrida, *Of Grammatology*, trans. Gayatri Spivak, London, 1976, p.63

34 Ibid., p.65

35 *Positions*, p.43

36 Christopher Macann, 'Jacques Derrida's Theory of Writing and the Concept of the Trace', in *Journal of the British Society for Phenomenology*, vol.3 no.2, May 1972, p.199

37 J.G. Fichte, Letter to Schelling, 15 January 1802, in *Briefwechsel*, p.152

38 Translated by Willis Domingo as *Against Epistemology*, Oxford, Blackwell, 1982

39 Jacques Derrida, 'Structure, Sign and Play in the Human Sciences', in *Writing and Difference*, p.281

40 *Against Epistemology*, p.23

41 Ibid., p.183

Index